SOFT, ROUND, AND BITLESS

Also by Ali Kermeen

The Working Equitation Training Manual

SOFT, ROUND, AND BITLESS

HOW TO TRAIN OR TRANSITION YOUR HORSE FOR COMPETITION OR PLEASURE

ALI KERMEEN

Trafalgar Square

First published in 2025 by
Trafalgar Square Books
The Stable Book Group, Brooklyn, New York

Copyright © 2025 Ali Kermeen

All rights reserved. No part of this book may be reproduced, by any means, without written permission of the publisher, except by a reviewer quoting brief excerpts for a review in a magazine, newspaper, or website.

Disclaimer of Liability
The author and publisher shall have neither liability nor responsibility to any person or entity with respect to any loss or damage caused or alleged to be caused directly or indirectly by the information contained in this book. While the book is as accurate as the author can make it, there may be errors, omissions, and inaccuracies.

Trafalgar Square Books encourages the use of approved safety helmets in all equestrian sports and activities.

Trafalgar Square Books certifies that the content in this book was generated by a human expert on the subject, and the content was edited, fact-checked, and proofread by human publishing specialists with a lifetime of equestrian knowledge. TSB does not publish books generated by artificial intelligence (AI).

Library of Congress Cataloging-in-Publication Data is available on file.
ISBN: 9781646012688

All photographs by Kathy Colman except pp. 51, 52, 59, 62, 64, 82, and 94 *top* (by Hollie Cower) and p. 7 (by Maria Marriott Photography).

Book design by Lauryl Eddlemon
Cover design by RM Didier
Index by Andrea Jones (JonesLiteraryServices.com)
Typeface: Myriad

Printed in China

10 9 8 7 6 5 4 3 2 1

For the Horses

CONTENTS

Introduction	1
What Does It Mean to Be Soft and Round?	6
How Do We Achieve This Without the Bit?	8
What Are the Benefits of Bitless Riding?	9
Drawbacks of Bitless Riding	11
PART 1: GROUNDWORK	**13**
Choosing Equipment for Groundwork	14
The Right Halter	14
The Right Lead Rope or Longe Line	15
A Whip, Stick, or Flag	17
Groundwork Fundamentals	**18**
Rope Handling and Leading Skills	18
Draw and Drive	18
Leading Position	19
Longeing Position	22
Energy Control	25
Moving Your Energy	26
Moving Together	27
Walking Together	27
Stopping Together	29
Backing Up Together	30
Asking for Movement in Different Ways and Directions	30
Follow a Feel	30
Gesture to Go	33
Shoo!	36

Back Up	36
Poll Flexions	39
Shoulder Yield	43
Arm Yield	44
Draw to Stop	46
Haunches Yield	49
Maestro	50
Shoulder Yield in Motion	52
Putting It All Together for Soft, Round Groundwork	**55**
Developing a Diagnostic Eye	55
Softening to the Hand	55
Poll Flexion in Motion	55
Neck Lowering	56
Rainbow	60
Raising the Withers	61
Balance	63
Range of Motion (ROM)	65
Magic in the Stillness	67

PART 2: EXPLORING BITLESS BRIDLES — 69

Bitless Bridle Parts and How They Fit	**70**
Anatomy and Fit	73
Material: Texture, Thickness, and Shape	75
Movement	75
Weight	76
Leverage	76
Types of Bitless Bridles	**78**
Traditional Hackamore	78
Mechanical Hackamore	88
S Hackamore	92

Sidepull	92
Cross-Under	95
Cavesson	96
Combination	98
Modifications	**98**

PART 3: CONNECTING BITLESS GROUNDWORK TO BITLESS RIDDEN WORK — 101

Transitioning to the Saddle	**102**
Riding Position Reminders	102
Mounting Block Etiquette	103
Groundwork Exercises Become Ridden Exercises	106
Poll Flexions to Ridden Flexions	*106*
Backing Up from the Ground to Rein-Back in the Saddle	*108*
Arm Yield to Leg-Yield	*111*
Haunches Yield to Rein Yield	*113*
Maestro to Ridden Maestro	*114*
Improving Contact and Connection	**116**
Feeling Bend	116
Shifting Lateral Balance	*118*
Feeling Roundness	118
Ridden Neck Lowering	*118*
Feeling Longitudinal Balance	121
Balance Up	*121*
Carrying On	124
Frequently Asked Questions	**125**
Conclusion	**131**
Acknowledgments	**133**
Index	**135**

97

105

INTRODUCTION

I started riding bitless in the 1990s, on my first horse, a teenaged black Thoroughbred named High Caliber. He had quirky ground manners, questionable conformation, and fell squarely into the "serviceably sound" category. He was perfect to me. I loved him the way a horse-crazy tween loves her first horse. Cal was nice enough to indulge me in whatever antic or discipline I wanted to try, with varied success.

We were at a serious eventing barn, and our rides fell into one of two categories: we were either working on skills we needed to be eventers, or we were just goofing off. When we were having a serious ride, Cal wore a saddle and a bridle. I remember that serious riding was much louder than the bitless riding; when wearing a bit, Cal would grind his teeth constantly.

But when we were goofing off, Cal wore nothing but a leather halter and lead rope. His neck and withers were so long that my 8-foot lead rope couldn't be made into usable reins, so I just held the rope on one side of his neck. These rides were peaceful and quiet, without Cal's teeth grinding. Looking back, it's clear to me that these "goofing off" rides were just as important as the rides where we worked on technique—and maybe even more effective for developing a seat and communication with a horse.

I didn't receive any instruction on bitless riding. At the time, I assumed all the control I could hope for was to be able to steer and stop my horse. I had never seen a serious rider go without a bit. Keep in mind this was a time before the internet, so I was only exposed to what I saw in person, as were all the people around me. None of us had seen "refined riding" done bitless.

After college, I took a job working at the same serious eventing barn where I grew up. One of my clients had a chestnut Thoroughbred named Shotgun Jack, who had a long career competing in Australia, New Zealand, and Japan as a steeplechaser, before being retrained as an event horse and imported to the United States. Jack had lovely training, but if the rein contact was dropped while he was aimed at a jump, he went very fast. If a light contact was maintained, all would be well.

We had a great time with Jack—until he developed a dangerous behavior. As he lifted off the ground to clear a jump, at the exact moment his rider rose out of the saddle, Jack violently raised his neck and flipped his head. This resulted in rider and horse having a "meeting of the minds," coconut-ing the rider's face against Jack's poll.

I thought this problem might have something to do with Jack's mouth, but I couldn't see anything wrong when I looked in it. I decided to run an experiment and try jumping Jack in a halter. After all, I had jumped Cal in a halter all the time when I was a kid. By now it was the early 2000s, and I had been exposed to more training techniques and methods, including some natural horsemanship. I figured I might have enough control if I used my rope halter. It had an 11-foot rope on it—long enough to loop around and make reins. Already, this was feeling like a more sophisticated apparatus than what I'd ridden Cal in.

I hopped on and tested my steering and stopping at a walk, trot, and canter. I seemed to have adequate control, so I decided to jump a cross-rail. That single cross-rail gave me two important pieces of data: First, even without contact, Jack didn't flip his head while jumping when in a halter. Second, it takes a long time to stop an ex-steeplechaser in a halter! After the jump, Jack opened up his stride; I could steer, but it took 12 large circles before I could slow Jack down. I ended our ride knowing that I had discovered part of a solution. But I wasn't sure what to do next.

My boss suggested trying a hybrid setup she had been using on her sensitive upper-level event horse. We took the noseband off Jack's snaffle bridle and replaced it with a "jumping cavesson"—a stiff rope noseband covered in leather, with steel rings attached on either side. I would hold one set of reins connected to the cavesson, and a second set of reins connected to the snaffle. In this way, I could keep contact on the cavesson on the way to a jump, but still have the snaffle to influence Jack on the landing side (fig. I.1).

Jack did well in this setup for several months. He was just as good in it on cross-country as he was in the arena. But occasionally, Jack's head flipping would come back, especially when he was nervous, so his

Wolf Teeth and Canine Teeth

Wolf teeth, not to be confused with canine teeth, are not present in all horses. If a horse does have wolf teeth, they erupt in front of the first cheek teeth, right behind where the bit sits. A horse can have anywhere from zero to four wolf teeth. They can erupt from the gums at varying heights, or remain below the gums unerupted. For a horse with wolf teeth—whether erupted or unerupted—a bit can be quite painful, even when used gently. (Canine teeth erupt in most male horses between four and five years old and are situated just behind the incisors. They do not commonly cause issues with the bit.)

I.1 Schooling cross-country on Shotgun Jack in his jumping cavesson and snaffle. (Note: The breastplate in this photo is poorly fitted to the point of being hazardous.)

owner decided to get an x-ray of his skull. It revealed two large bone spurs in Jack's lower jaw, near where the bit sits. These bony growths were causing him pain, which he was trying to alleviate by flipping his head.

Around the same time, I had another client with a young draft cross named Blackie who was heavy in the bridle. When met with bit pressure, he often opened his mouth and shook his head. A trainer friend of mine noticed he still had his wolf teeth.

We decided to try an English-style mechanical hackamore on Blackie until we could get his wolf teeth extracted and allow time for healing. Unlike Jack's jumping cavesson, Blackie's mechanical hackamore had 4-inch-long metal shanks on the sides, a wide leather piece padded with fleece over the nose, and a curb chain under the jaw. This design gives the rider more leverage than a simple halter or jumping cavesson. Blackie didn't open his mouth in the hackamore, and we could steer and stop in it, but there wasn't much refinement.

After Blackie healed up, he went back to wearing a bit and was able to improve his contact and connection. (I actually saw Blackie in 2024, 20 years after his wolf teeth extraction. I found out he'd ended up having a long, successful career as a dressage horse, all the way through Prix St. Georges!)

Shortly after my reintroduction to bitless riding, I badly injured my wrist and left my job at the eventing barn. I moved my personal horse to a large boarding barn closer to my house with 200 horses. Many riders at the new barn exclusively rode on trails and never used the arenas. There were English riders, Western riders, trail riders, and even jousting riders! There were folks who trick trained their horses, and people who didn't ride their horses at all.

Sharing space with so many horses being ridden in so many ways was new for me. It was a physical manifestation of the way the equestrian internet was developing. I saw different kinds of horsemanship, without actively searching them out. Folks rode in all kinds of bridles. Some had very harsh-looking bits, some rode in snaffles, some rode bitless, and a few even rode bridle-less.

After my injury, I continued to have trouble using my left hand. Through a friend, I was introduced to Ellen Eckstein, a Grand Prix rider who also coached para-equestrians. When I met her, Ellen had a one-handed student making a bid for the World Equestrian Games (WEG) in para dressage, so it made sense that she could help me too.

Ellen took principles that she learned from working with natural horsemanship trainer Tom Dorrance for 30 years and applied them to dressage. I had studied some natural horsemanship before, but only as something that was done separately from dressage, not as part of dressage itself. Working with Ellen changed my perspective about riding and training horses; she taught me it doesn't matter what the eventual intended use of the horse is going to be, all horses need to be trained to "speak" the same language as their riders. This language can be universal among disciplines.

It ultimately took seven years to heal my wrist, and I finally was well enough to start training other people's horses again. In those years, I had met many wonderful horsemen, each with their own unique styles of training, and I became more receptive to different ways to keep horses happier in their work. I willingly trained any horse, regardless of discipline. I started to loosen nosebands and dropped snaffle bits lower so the corners of the horse's mouth no longer held wrinkles while the reins were slack. But despite these changes, for a while, if a horse came to me in a bitless bridle, I still insisted on using a bit.

One of my clients was interested in Cowboy Dressage, which, at the time, was still a fledgling discipline that highlighted elements of Western riding traditions and classical dressage. I started going with her to Cowboy Dressage gatherings. It was there that I first saw horses that were soft, round, and bitless (I explain what I mean by the terms "soft" and "round" beginning on p. 6).

As a whole, these horses were much more relaxed and had softer facial expressions than what I was seeing at traditional dressage shows. The horses in hackamores particularly stood out to me. They were able to respond to their riders' subtle cues for flexion and bending in a way I previously thought was difficult or impossible to do without the help of a bit.

One day, while waiting for my class to be called in one of my first Cowboy Dressage shows, I found myself alone

Historically Bitless

Some historians think bitless bridles were used as early as 4000 BCE. Archaeological evidence of bitless riding is questionable at best, since the materials used to make bitless bridles were composed of natural fibers that did not withstand the test of time. Artistic evidence shows use of bitless bridles in 1400 BCE.

In 400 BCE, Xenophon was influenced by Persian horsemen who used a thick noseband with a rein attached to the top. This type of noseband, called a *hakma*, was derived from the bridle used on camels.

When the Spanish colonized the West Coast of North America in the 1700s, *jáquimas* were developed in response to a shortage of metal. Today, we know the *jáquima* as a hackamore.

in the arena with Phil Monaghan. Phil is an Australian trainer specializing in training horses in hackamores; that day, his horse was wearing a thin hackamore, with a bridle on top of it. I sidled my horse next to his, introduced myself, and for the next 40 minutes, fired away questions, all of which he graciously answered. I've never felt so fortunate to have to wait around for something before!

Fueled by the education Phil gave me, I dove into the hackamore world, studying with any experts I could find, and reading what little material was out there about the art of using a hackamore. What I learned was a mixed bag. In some of the most widely available books on hackamores, there were descriptions of techniques I did not feel were particularly kind to horses, while I also found information that was very helpful. I also learned that riding in a bitless bridle predated the invention of a bit, and in paintings, I saw classical dressage depicted in a curb bit, with a second rein attached to the headstall noseband. It turned out the hybrid bit/bitless bridle I'd tried on Shotgun Jack had been around for centuries.

I experimented with equipment and techniques on the horses I was riding and found that the hackamore was a better tool than the bit for some of them. I found places where riding with the hackamore complemented the work I had done with Ellen Eckstein, and overlayed nicely on my traditional dressage foundation.

Not every horse preferred the hackamore, but some really thrived in it. I started taking more horses to the Cowboy Dressage shows, since I felt the goals of Cowboy Dressage better aligned with what I wanted out of a riding horse than modern competitive dressage. Sometimes, but not all the time, I competed horses at these shows in hackamores. I had success in my new discipline, winning the gaited division at Cowboy Dressage World Finals on three different horses. Two of those horses competed in traditional hackamores.

Learning to be effective without a bit has made me a better rider when I use a bit. I like my horses to be what is described as *soft* and *round*, no matter what they have on their face. I have a series of exercises that I use for all horses, regardless of their eventual use, which sets them up to understand how to be soft and round. I'm happy to be able to share them with you in this book, along with considerations for choosing the best bitless bridle for you and your horse. But first, let me explain what *soft* and *round* mean, and why they are desirable in a riding horse.

WHAT DOES IT MEAN TO BE SOFT AND ROUND?

A *soft* horse responds willingly to the lightest of cues from the rider, without physical or mental tension. He might appear to be working directly from the rider's thoughts, with imperceptible aids. You won't see a soft horse bracing against a rider, and chances are you will see this soft horse paired with a soft rider.

A soft rider uses subtle and effective aids that don't offend her horse. She is slow to take up pressure on the reins and has excellent timing to release quickly when appropriate. Her neutral riding position is light and free of prolonged tension. A soft horse and rider produce a picture of harmony and understanding (fig. I.2). They work as a partnership.

I.2 Johnny Bug is soft, round, and bitless while competing in Cowboy Dressage.

A horse that is *round* uses his body in the most optimal way to support the weight of a rider. He bears weight fairly equally on all four legs. His abdominal muscles are working, his back is lifted, and his thoracic sling is engaged. His body is aligned on the track he is traveling on, unless he is asked to perform lateral work. His neck is arched, which places his face just in front of vertical. Improvement in any one of these areas helps the others. This focus on balance, straightness, and posture is beneficial to his longevity as a riding horse.

A horse that can carry his own body in this frame, without being forced, is able to be athletic and is in an ideal position to be influenced by the rider. The rider will find it easier to ride a round horse. His gaits will be softer than if he was traveling with a stiff back and braced neck. A soft, round horse is a joy to ride in any discipline.

HOW DO WE ACHIEVE THIS WITHOUT THE BIT?

If you want to teach a horse to be soft, you must first be a soft rider. Soft riders are not passive riders; they "firm up" when it is required. A soft rider has clear and consistent boundaries with her horse. This requires having a picture or feeling of what she wants to accomplish with her horse, and an intellectual understanding of what to do to elicit the desired results. She will be able to control each part of her body independently and be deliberate with her movements. This self-control extends to her internal energy as well.

To encourage a horse to be round, you must be a balanced rider. You do not want to brace on your reins or grip with your legs in order to stay on your horse. You need to have the horse's face and the sides of his body available for clear communication from the rider in regards to bend, straightness, and energy.

Horses are content to just be horses. They don't inherently know what it is to be a dressage horse, a trail horse, or any other kind of specialization we assign to them. They have feelings about what feels balanced, comfortable, easy and difficult in their own bodies. They don't have a picture in their heads of what an ideal posture looks like for a specialized horse. That image exists solely in the rider's head. It is through the art of horsemanship that you can form a language with your horse to explain to him what it is that you want him to do in order to be closer to the ideal picture in your mind.

As you are training your horse to be soft, it is important that you and your horse share a common language. You will want your horse to respond to small cues he understands, rather than being manhandled into positions that don't readily make sense to him. Horses and riders both need to understand this language, which is much more complex than simply kicking and pulling.

Watch horses interact with one another. Do you see kicking and biting? In a harmonious herd, you will not. The horses seem to move in a synchronized way that is informed by different postures, gestures, and what can sometimes appear to be a collective consciousness. *This* is the language your horse knows how to speak. He is willing to try to learn a common language with you, but it is important you are respectful enough that you don't inadvertently threaten or offend him in his language. Instead, we can use elements of the way horses interact with each other to create the language between you and your horse.

Choosing to ride with a bit, bitless, or bridleless is like speaking different dialects of the common language you create with your horse. In order to be successful riding bitless, you and your horse must first learn to be fluent in this common language.

WHAT ARE THE BENEFITS OF BITLESS RIDING?

Have you looked inside your horse's mouth? What does his mouth look like compared to other horses? Does he have any scarring or malformations on his tongue? How about on his lips? How many canine teeth or wolf teeth does he have (see p. 2)? What's the distance between the corner of his mouth and his premolar? What's the distance between the corner of his mouth and his canine teeth? Does he have a high palate or a low palate? Does he have a thick tongue or a thin tongue? A wide tongue or a narrow tongue? Are the bars of his mouth flat or angled? Does he have thin lips or fleshy lips? Does he have any bruising on the bars of his mouth? When he wears a bit, have you noted signs that indicate he might be sensitive or allergic to particular metals?

These are all questions that a good horseman will take into account when selecting a bit for a horse in any discipline. Examining a horse's mouth might reveal factors that could produce communication issues or pain while wearing a bit. However, the most important factor to consider is how the horse feels about the bit. Some horses with mouths that might not be ideally conformed for carrying a bit may seem to be happy enough wearing one. But more often, they are unhappy in a bit (more on this in a moment). Some horses with theoretically "ideal" mouths for bitting never seem happy with the bit in their mouth. Ultimately, the decision if the horse should be wearing a bit, or go bitless, should be up to the horse.

How do we know if the horse is unhappy with a bit? Even the mildest of bits are capable of causing a horse pain, because mouth tissues are extremely sensitive. Evaluate your horse with a fresh eye and answer eight questions.

THE BIT COMFORT ASSESSMENT

☐ **1** Is your horse difficult to bridle?

☐ **2** Does his mouth carry tension, like pulled back lips, exposed teeth, or a "hard" chin (tension clearly observable) while he is wearing his bit?

☐ **3** Does he open his mouth or stick out his tongue while he is wearing a bit?

☐ **4** Does he grind, clack, or gnash his teeth when wearing a bit?

☐ **5** Is his movement less free, especially with his hind legs, when he is wearing a bit?

☐ **6** Does he have trouble keeping a steady rein contact with the bit?

☐ **7** Does he toss his head, duck behind the vertical, or come above the bit?

☐ **8** Does he lock or cross his jaw when wearing a bit?

If you answered yes to any of the eight questions in the test, your horse might not be happy wearing the bit you are currently using, or possibly, any bit at all. It is worth trying a bitless option, if for no other reason than to see if the issue is with the bit, with another aspect of his equipment, or with his rider. Try a bitless option, and see if there is improvement in any of these eight areas. I've seen improvements in each of these areas by transitioning a horse from a bit to a bitless bridle, and I've also tried bitless with some horses who ended up preferring the bit. Regardless of the end result, I have never regretted trying a bitless option. Anything you can do for your horse to try to make him happier and free from pain is worth doing.

DRAWBACKS OF BITLESS RIDING

One drawback of riding bitless is that many competitions do not allow horses to compete bitless. Rules about bitless bridle use depend on the sport and the relevant governing body. Some disciplines have no restrictions at all about what the horse is wearing on his face. Some disciplines allow horses to compete in certain styles of bitless bridles but not others. Some disciplines allow horses under a certain age to compete in a bosal-style hackamore, with the understanding that "bitless" is a step in training toward eventual performance in a bitted bridle. Some disciplines allow reins attached to a bitless headstall, as long as the horse also has reins attached to a bit. Other disciplines strictly forbid the use of bitless bridles altogether.

Riding bitless can feel like a leap of faith because of a perceived lack of control versus riding with a bit. But most of the time, the control over a horse has more to do with training and partnership, and less to do with equipment. Horses can bolt in bitless or bitted bridles. They can drop their heads and graze in both styles of

It's All Connected

Through equine cadaver dissection, scientists have discovered several interesting biomechanical phenomena related to pressure on the horse's tongue and movement of the limbs. First, when downward pressure is applied to the cadaver's tongue, the hind legs are not able to be moved as freely as when there is no pressure on the tongue. Next, some scientists report they can feel the tongue of a cadaver horse move when the fascia over the stifle is manipulated. Others have suggested the restriction of the tongue inhibiting the movement of the limbs is related to the connection of the tongue to the hyoid bone of the skull, which is in turn connected to the limbs through various muscle chains. Anecdotally, I've noticed a parallel phenomenon in some ridden horses, who are more active with their hind legs when ridden bitless compared to when they are ridden with a bitted bridle.

bridle as well. There are bitless bridles that can have effects that are just as severe as bitted bridles. When causing pain is what someone wants to do to their horse to ensure compliance (I hope not), they can find a way to do that whether riding bitless or bitted.

To that end, it is important to learn to use your tools correctly. Going bitless isn't going to solve all your training problems if your horse lacks understanding about what your cues mean. It's also not going to solve a rider's coordination or timing inadequacies. However, certain bitless bridles, when adjusted correctly, may lessen the potential for injuries to the horse caused by uneducated riders.

If your horse wears a bit and you are curious about going bitless, it is tempting to put your new bitless bridle on and ride the same way as you did with the bit. Although you will probably be able to get away with doing that, and ride easily from Point A to Point B, it is also likely you won't have the same responsiveness and ability to work your horse in a soft round manner this way. Often, riders find that bitless works at first, but then their horse becomes more resistant to the bitless bridle over time, because they don't understand there are different nuances between riding with a bit and bitless. This book will show you how to successfully transition from riding with a bit, to riding without a bit, while enhancing your communication with the horse so that he can be a safe, willing, and happy athletic partner.

PART 1

GROUNDWORK

....

IT STARTS ON THE GROUND

Whenever you use a new piece of equipment on your horse, it is best to check out how your horse feels about it from the ground before you get on his back. Your horse is already used to wearing a halter, and is probably used to wearing a bridle, so the bitless bridle should not feel foreign to him. Nevertheless, since we rely heavily on our bridle to communicate with our horses, it is only fair to your horse to show him what the different sensations on his face are supposed to mean to him. Make sure you and your horse have a common language that includes all the equipment you will be using before attempting ridden exercises.

Chances are that you and your horse can already do most of the groundwork in this section. But it is equally probable that there is a hole in your—or your horse's—education. Going through <u>all</u> the groundwork exercises in the pages that follow is going to show where those holes are, so we can kick some dirt in them, and then build a strong foundation on top of them. Try all these exercises, in the order prescribed, to make sure you are laying your foundation on solid ground. Do these exercises even if you are sure that you will be successful. Returning to basics is always worthwhile.

> If you are new to groundwork, it is never too late to start! Groundwork is a worthwhile tool to establish a common language and a relationship with a horse. Riders who can't do groundwork are like drivers who can't change the oil in their own cars.

CHOOSING EQUIPMENT FOR GROUNDWORK

Groundwork equipment is meant to teach the horse and rider the language they will use when doing ridden work, but first in a safer scenario, with the rider on foot. To the horse, the cues taught in a halter from the ground should feel like the cues given in the bridle from the saddle. Ideally, equipment minimizes the difference in feeling between halter/lead rope and bridle/reins. Your personal preferences in selecting groundwork and riding equipment may be different than mine, and that is totally fine. Your horsemanship should be your own. Just be sure that you know why you like your groundwork equipment and how it will relate to your riding equipment. Knowing this will ensure your groundwork improves your ridden work.

I have strong preferences for what equipment pairs well with my horsemanship style. I've thought about each element on its own, and how it relates to the horse, the handler, and other pieces of equipment.

THE RIGHT HALTER

I prefer a medium-stiff rope halter that fits the horse's head well (fig. 1.1). A halter that is too soft can give a wishy-washy cue. A halter that is too stiff can be uncomfortable for the horse at rest. I choose halters without metal rings joining the components. Metal rings interfere with the directionality and intensity of my cues.

The noseband should be adjusted so that it rests on top of the nasal bone, not on the delicate cartilage below (fig. 1.2). Check this by feeling down your horse's face. You can determine where the nasal bone ends and the cartilage begins because there is a distinct difference in hardness. If you have sensitive fingers, you can even feel facial nerves and veins. If your horse seems bothered by pressure on these structures, try not to have your halter sit on those areas while at rest.

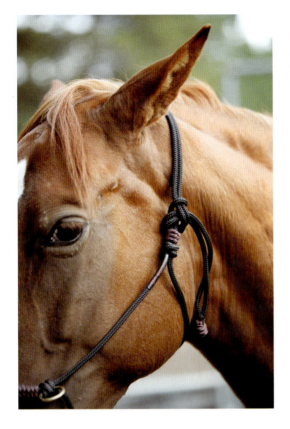

1.1 The rope halter should be tied or fastened so that it will not loosen during movement. Achieve this by tying the crownpiece around the loop of the halter, as pictured. People often make the mistake of tying the crownpiece back to itself, which will make your halter loosen during use.

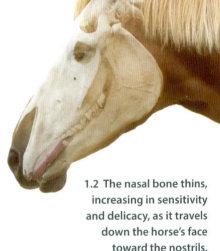

1.2 The nasal bone thins, increasing in sensitivity and delicacy, as it travels down the horse's face toward the nostrils.

THE RIGHT LEAD ROPE OR LONGE LINE

When I'm communicating with the horse from the ground, I want him to feel the exact amount of push or pull that I apply to his equipment. Having a snap connecting the halter and lead rope disrupts the communication. The horse will feel the weight of the snap, especially when he is in motion and the snap is swinging. It is easier to establish a clear communication if you remove the snap from your lead rope. In this way, you and your horse feel each other more clearly (figs. 1.3 A & B). You wouldn't put a heavy snap between your bridle and reins when riding, so don't use one between the halter and lead rope when working on the ground.

I also avoid snaps after seeing the damage they can do to a horse's teeth. Some trainers swing the lead rope and hit the horse in the face. If the snap is on the part that swings, it can chip teeth and bruise flesh. Since people rarely look

1.3 A & B A lovely leather halter and lead rope suited for casual leading and tying is shown in Photo A. I'm using the rope to try to push Rosie's head away from me, and the snap disrupts the feel I'm trying to convey.

A quality lead rope for groundwork will be a bit thicker and stiffer where it ties into the halter, as shown in Photo B. The stiffness of the rope in this section allows you to push the halter away from you, communicating your direction to the horse. A rope that is limp, or has a snap, will not allow you to have this action of influence available to you during your groundwork. Ropes like this are often sold with snaps looped on to the ends that can be easily removed immediately after purchase. (Note that once the rope is broken in, it is harder to remove the snap.)

in their horse's mouths, and their horse's skin is covered with hair, these injuries often go unnoticed.

I want a lead rope that is pliable in my hands but becomes stiff in the last 10 inches where it connects to the halter. The stiff section of rope will enable you to use it to give a pushing sensation on the side of the horse's face closest to you, instead of only connecting with his face on the opposite side. This compensates for the difference between one lead rope and two reins. On the other end of the rope, I like a leather "popper." The popper allows me to feel when I'm getting to the end of the rope and helps the rope twirl when needed as a visual aid. (It's harder to twirl the end of the rope when it is heavy with a knot or piece of rubber.)

When I'm teaching groundwork skills to folks who are new at it, I start with a 12-foot rope, and we mostly work at a walk. When we start to do more trotting and cantering, we shift to a 25-foot rope with the same properties as our shorter rope. Since I don't like snaps, and knots connecting to the halter can be difficult to undo, I simply have one halter connected to a 12-foot rope, and a second halter connected to the 25-foot rope (similar to a longe line).

A WHIP, STICK, OR FLAG

I usually don't use a whip when I'm doing groundwork. Instead, typically my horses are attuned to my energy (more on this on p. 25), and I can use the leather popper on the end of my rope if I need to motivate the horse further. However, I will carry a longe whip (a "horseman's stick" or "flag" can also be used) if I need to "extend my arm" to reach the horse. This might happen if I need to teach a horse to keep a greater distance from me while circling, or if the horse lacks responsiveness to driving cues. If you feel safer doing groundwork with a whip, then use a whip.

GROUNDWORK FUNDAMENTALS

Once you have your equipment selected, it's time to use it to create a language with your horse on the ground. We will then be able to easily transfer this groundwork language to a ridden language. The following exercises start off very basic, and then build skills off one another. As I mentioned before, start with the first exercise and do all the exercises in order, even if you think that you and your horse have already mastered them. Make sure you can perform every one of these skills from the horse's left and right sides. If you are struggling to achieve results in any exercise, review the prerequisites, and make sure they are solid.

ROPE HANDLING AND LEADING SKILLS

To be an effective communicator with your horse, you need to be able to use your equipment like an extension of your body. This means you need to learn to use your equipment properly, *before* you put it on your horse. Practicing your rope handling skills without your horse will improve your dexterity and fluidity. You also have freedom to fumble as you learn new skills and hand positions with your rope. When you are ready to add your horse to the conversation, you will be less likely to create unintentional signals with your equipment that will confuse him.

■ Draw and Drive

Start with your halter hung on a dangling hook and your lead line in your hands (note that in the photos, I have used a model horse skull to give the halter shape, but this is not necessary—an empty halter hanging from a hook is fine). As you move your hands to different positions, try to keep the halter from swinging. First, identify your *leading* hand and your *driving* hand: when you are facing the same direction as your halter (the same position as you would be if it was on your horse), the hand *nearest the halter* is your leading hand, and the hand *farthest from the halter* is your driving hand (fig. 1.4). When you are at a 90-degree angle from your halter, as you would be while longeing your horse in a circle around you, the hand *closest to the horse's head* is your leading hand, and the hand *closest to the horse's tail* is your driving hand.

Your leading hand should be soft around the rope, allowing it to easily slide through. Your driving hand holds the excess rope firmly in loops that lay over the hand, instead of encircling it. Loops laid over the hand are less likely to cause an injury if the horse pulls away. Be sure to have enough rope between your leading and driving hands so that there can be a droop to the rope, but not so much droop that you step on or trip over the rope.

■ Leading Position

In leading position, you and your horse are facing the same way (fig. 1.4). The two of you will be traveling at the same speed, and your leading hand is oriented so that your thumb is the highest point. Your hands are soft, and your leading hand is open when "cruising." Still just using the halter hanging on a hook, try these exercises:

> **Draw vs. Drive**
>
> Drawing a horse is when you get a horse to move toward you. Driving a horse is moving the horse away from you. Every exercise we are going to do has an element of drive, draw, or both.

1 We almost always see images of horses being led from the left (near) side. I want to also lead from the right (off) side. Every horse and rider should be able to do both. Leading from the right helps horses that have a hard time bending right, longeing to the right, and accepting novel objects from the right. Try changing sides and your leading and driving hands.

2 Practice changing the length of the rope between your soft leading hand and the halter by using the driving hand to push and pull the rope through your grip.

3 Use your leading hand to push the halter forward, then let the line go slack again. Now, push the halter away from you. This should work if your lead rope has a stiff section closest to the halter.

4 Use your driving hand to twirl the rope in front of the halter. Can you twirl without moving the halter? Train yourself to twirl the rope clockwise if your left hand is your driving hand, and counterclockwise if your right hand is the driving hand. This will allow the horse to see the rope as it comes toward him from above, rather than having the rope come toward him from below, which would be an unfair surprise.

5 Can you keep the halter still while you use your driving hand behind your body? In this position, the excess rope can be flapped instead of twirled (fig. 1.5).

1.4 This is the default leading position when on the horse's right side. In this moment, my left hand is the *leading* hand, and my right hand is the *driving* hand. I am standing evenly with or just behind where the rope connects to the halter. There is slack in the rope between my leading hand and the halter. Both my hands are softly open, but ready to firm up if necessary. My shoulders are relaxed, and my energy is down.

This posture on the ground is important to become a soft rider and develop a soft horse from the saddle. For safety, I do not have my excess rope looped around my driving hand. I'm carrying it in a loop short enough that I won't trip on it, but long enough that I can easily increase my distance from the horse without fumbling with lots of extra loops or accidentally pulling on the halter.

1.5 I am flapping the rope behind me where it might contact the horse's body. It is important that you can do this while you are looking forward, not at your flapping rope. Be sure to keep your leading hand soft and your fingers light. This allows you to stabilize the connection to the halter, but leaves you ready to open your hand a bit when the horse moves forward. This ensures your horse doesn't receive backward pressure on the halter at the same time he's being driven forward, which could confuse him. If you have good timing with your release, you can apply forward pressure with your leading hand, but be sure to drop the pressure *as soon* as your horse comes forward.

■ Longeing Position

Longeing position is when you are working your horse on a circle moving around you at a distance (fig. 1.6). The following exercises will help you influence your horse when he is farther away from you than in leading position. From longeing position, you will also be able to see more of your horse, since you will be facing his side. This allows you to evaluate your horse's posture and make changes while he's in motion.

> **Lungeing, Longeing, and Lounging**
>
> In English, we refer to the act of moving a horse in a circle around us on a long line as "longeing." This term originated from the French term *allonge*, which is used to describe the lengthening of the rope. Often, the term is spelled "lungeing," and occasionally, you will see someone spell it "lounging," which almost makes sense too. A chaise longue is French for "long chair." In the 1800s, English speakers mixed up the letters of chaise longue, and we started referring to these chairs as chaise lounge; the spelling made sense, so it stuck. Now we simply call them "lounge chairs."
> When I'm talking horses, I like to spell the action as "longeing" because it makes me think of the original intent of the phrase. I try not to be distracted by the thought of horses working out, doing lunges and squats, or horses sipping piña coladas in their lounge chairs.

1.6 This is your default longeing position. I am on the left side of the horse, so my left hand is the leading hand, and my right hand is the driving hand. Take note of the openness and softness of my leading hand—this allows for the finer movements that allow for connection and light contact. The driving hand has the responsibility of maintaining the length of rope. My weight is evenly distributed on my left and right feet, and my shoulders and arms are relaxed.

1 With your halter still hanging from a hook, switch from leading position to longeing position. If you are staying on the same side of your horse, your leading and driving hand will switch.

2 Sometimes your leading hand will be overhand, with your pinky finger closest to the halter. At other times, your leading hand will be underhand, with your index finger closest to the halter. Practice switching between overhand and underhand.

3 Position your leading hand overhand, and your driving hand underhand. Practice running your leading hand up and down the length of the rope, keeping it loose, while your driving hand adjusts the length of rope (fig. 1.7).

1.7 Here, I am sliding my leading hand down the rope, keeping my fingers soft and open. I have shortened the amount of line between my hand and the halter. This is the groundwork equivalent to shortening your reins when mounted. You should be able to do this skill smoothly and without fumbling. Your horse should only feel a difference in the contact if that is what you are intending. Notice that my eyes and body language are directing my horse forward, without blocking or restricting movement.

1.8 My leading hand stabilizes the length of rope attached to the horse's halter so I can "twirl" the driving end of the lead rope without the horse feeling a pull. This ensures that the horse is not receiving mixed messages from my driving hand and my leading hand.

1.9 "Rolling" the length of rope extending between the leading hand and driving hand is a handy tool for when you are trying to create distance between you and your horse's shoulder. Be sure you can perform this skill easily—as well as transition in and out of it—without moving your halter on the hook.

24 | SOFT, ROUND, AND BITLESS

4 Practice "twirling" the rope with your driving hand (fig. 1.8). Can you keep the halter still on the hook while you do so?

5 Practice "rolling" the excess rope between the leading hand and driving hand (fig. 1.9).

6 Use your open leading hand to push the rope across your body, toward where your horse's hip would be. As you are pushing on the rope, notice that the halter swings toward you. Finish by bringing your leading hand back to its original side (we will be doing this maneuver when we get to the Maestro exercise on p. 50).

7 While facing your halter, move it to your right with your leading hand (right hand). Return the halter to a neutral position, then smoothly switch your leading and driving hands. Now, move the halter to the left. Don't look at your hands or rope while changing hands.

ENERGY CONTROL

Have you ever had your horse respond to someone else's cue differently than he responds to your cue? It may seem like the other person is doing exactly the same thing but getting a different result. This can often happen when a more experienced person or trainer is handling or riding your horse. Why are they getting so much more out of your horse than you are? If you are doing the same cues with the same timing, then the answer is the difference in the person's energy.

The energy I'm referring to is what some old cowboys refer to as "life." You might hear one of them say "bring your life up" when encouraging someone to become more energized. Another word for this notion is "spirit." A horse with lots of energy is often described as "spirited." The word "spirit" is closely tied to breath via respiration—both words come from the Latin root word "*spir*" (which means *breathe*). Other cultures have names for this internal energy as well. It is referred to as *chi* in Chinese, *ki* in Japanese (as in aikido or reiki), and *prana* in Hinduism.

Master horsemen use their energy as an aid. They bring their energy up when they want to energize the horse and bring their energy down when they want to quiet their horse. You can learn to use your energy as an aid as well, and managing your energy is a crucial component of being soft. Intentionally moving your energy is what should happen *before* you use a rope, rein, or movement of your body to influence your horse. Horses are sensitive to energy; they use energy to communicate with each other constantly.

■ Moving Your Energy

You can do this next exercise anywhere, and you should practice it often. If you are new at moving your energy, make sure you start by securing your environment—find a quiet place, free from distraction.

1 Take three deep and slow breaths, concentrating on feeling your body. Feel the fabrics touching your skin. Feel your chest expand and contract as you breathe.

2 Identify seven spots along the centerline of your body and feel them individually. I like to think of the seven *chakras*: root, sacral, solar plexus, heart, throat, third eye, and crown. If you aren't familiar with these chakras, instead, identify a point at the bottom of your pelvis, then the spots below your navel, below your ribs, on your centerline near your heart, your throat, between your eyes, and the top of your head.

3 Place your awareness in your belly. See if you can sense if you feel more energetic near your navel, or near the bottom of your ribs. It helps me to visualize my energy as a thick glowing golden liquid with pink specks in it.

4 Now, concentrate on moving your energy *up*. As you inhale, feel your energy grow inside of you. It may help to actually move your body, or even jump up, as you lift your energy. How high do you feel it move? To your throat? To the top of your head? Hold your energy up for a few seconds.

5 Next, try to bring your energy all the way *down*. Exhale, and feel your energy sink into the bottom of your pelvis. Visualize it pooling at the bottom of your body. Dwell with your energy low for a few seconds.

6 Practice bringing your energy up and down twice more.

7 To complete the energy movement exercise, come to rest with your energy just below your ribs.

Learning to move your energy is like exercising a muscle. At first, it might be awkward and stiff to get your energy to move a little bit. But as you continue to practice, you will start moving your energy without all the preparatory steps. You will be able to adjust your energy easily while you are working with your horse.

MOVING TOGETHER

I'm assuming your horse is halter-broke, but how refined is your leading? For casual leading, and some groundwork, there are reasons to walk ahead of your horse, next to your horse and close, next to your horse at a distance, or even behind your horse as he walks ahead of you! I expect that my horse walks when I walk, stops when I stop, and backs up when I back up. All these things should be achieved with a completely loose lead rope. If you have to drag your horse along to get him to walk with you, or pull on him to stop, these issues need to be addressed before moving on.

The goal of this next exercise is that you and your horse start walking together, stop walking together, and back up together. Before you begin, make sure you have practiced the rope handling and leading skills (p.18) and energy exercise (p. 26) *without* your horse.

■ Walking Together

1 Standing on the left side of your haltered horse, facing the same direction as him, hold your hand directly below the junction of the lead rope and halter. If you want more distance from your horse, try to keep your leading hand in line with the junction of rope and halter, but carry it closer to your own body.

2 To start walking with your horse, bring up your energy as you take a step forward (fig. 1.10). Inhale as you begin to move, filling yourself with happy, lively energy. If your horse is eager to walk, you won't need to bring your energy up very much. If your horse tends to be sluggish, you will want your breath to feel like it is high in your chest, near your neck.

3 If your horse doesn't come along with you right away, you can ask him to move forward with your leading hand. If he still doesn't come forward, use your driving hand to reach behind you and flap your excess rope. If this still doesn't get your horse to walk forward, you can throw your excess rope behind you so it either hits

1.10 Rosie is responding to my request to walk forward with more energy. Notice that Rosie's eye is looking at the rope. She saw it coming and increased her energy to match mine, which you can see by looking at the synchronicity of Rosie's front legs with my legs. When I encouraged her forward, I kept my hands as soft as I could without changing the length of the rope. I also made sure to keep slack in the length of rope between my leading hand and the halter, so I wouldn't give a conflicting signal of pulling on the halter while simultaneously encouraging forward motion. Since Rosie and I are in sync with our energy levels, I won't give another flap of my excess rope, unless Rosie's energy level drops lower than mine again.

the ground or the horse. Remember to keep your eyes forward and your energy up as you are asking for forward movement.

As you are walking forward, keep slack in the line between your leading hand and the halter and your breath in "neutral position." The neutral position for your breath is in the middle of your trunk, somewhere between your navel and the bottom of your rib cage. If your horse lags behind, you can use the techniques outlined on pp. 33 and 36 to get him to put slack back in the line.

1.11 As I begin to stop, I can tell Rohan isn't paying attention. Because I suspect he will not stop his feet when I stop mine, I set a boundary by twirling the rope in front of us. Here, I have twirled the rope so he will see it come down from above and have a chance to slow down or stop before it contacts his nose. If I were to twirl the rope in the opposite direction, he wouldn't be able to see it before it connected with his lower jaw, and that wouldn't be fair to him.

■ Stopping Together

1 To halt your horse, bring your energy down as you exhale and stop your feet. Think of "dimming" your energy and making it still. Your breath will feel like it is low in your belly, well below your navel.

2 If your horse doesn't stop with you, twirl your excess rope in front of both of you with your driving hand (fig. 1.11). If he doesn't stop, he will walk into the twirling rope. Stand your ground and don't let your horse pull you along.

■ Backing Up Together

1 To back your horse up, continue facing the same way as your horse, bring your breath up again, and start to step backward.

2 If your horse doesn't immediately come with you, do not turn around to face him or pull him back with the rope. Instead, twirl your rope in front of you. If he doesn't match your steps backward, he will run into your rope. When this is a new concept for him, reward the small tries with a release of pressure. If he shifts his weight back, that's an excellent start! After a couple successful repetitions of a weight shift, begin to expect the horse to move one step back. Pause and reward your horse before you have to correct him whenever possible.

Whenever you are leading your horse, practice achieving this level of refinement . Always adjust your energy before cuing him. Your energy should be your primary aid whenever you are working with your horse, and the overall goal is for your horse to tune in and respond to your energy coming up and down. Energetic shifts are how horses communicate with each other before resorting to biting and kicking. They are also how soft humans communicate with their horses before resorting to kicking and pulling. As you are developing common language with your horse, you need to meet him halfway in the language he already speaks with other horses by having control over your own energy. With practice, ideally, you will never have to take the slack out of your rope or do any twirling or flapping.

ASKING FOR MOVEMENT IN DIFFERENT WAYS AND DIRECTIONS

■ Follow a Feel

Now that leading is going well, and your horse is responsive to your energy, let's start to have him put out more energy than you do! "Following a feel" is when you can influence your horse to move in a different direction than his handler.

Again, before we begin this new exercise, we need to be sure our previous skills are secure. These include the longeing positions discussed earlier (see p. 22), and the Moving Together exercises (p. 27).

1 Our goal is to teach the horse to move forward by following a gentle pressure on the rope. Start at the halt and get into longeing position, meaning you will be facing your horse's rib cage. Your goal is to remain stationary while the horse moves forward.

2 Place your leading hand in overhand position and extend it forward and to the side, slowly taking the slack out of the line, adding forward pressure if needed (fig. 1.12). Aim your shoulders toward the horse's haunches and increase your energy, until the horse takes a step in the direction of the line.

3 If he doesn't follow the feel of the rope forward, encourage him to move by twirling your rope in your driving hand.

4 As soon as your horse moves in the correct direction, allow the slack to come back to the line and your leading arm to return to a more relaxed position at your side.

At this point, assess if your horse understood what was being asked of him as you encouraged him to follow a feel. If he understood and acted like he's followed a feel a hundred times before, great! Allow him to continue moving around you (fig. 1.13). Now you are officially longeing!

If your horse did not respond to following a feel, allow him to come to a stop as soon as he takes a step in the right direction. Tell him he's good, breathe with him for a moment, then ask him to follow a feel again. Your goal is to simply get him better at following a feel than when you first started the session. That's it! Longeing will come on another day.

Good Timing

When doing groundwork, keep in mind that you are also teaching your horse how to respond to cues when he is being ridden. Whenever you take the slack out of the rope, do so slowly, giving your horse a chance to respond to slight pressure before you escalate into a pull or push. Once the horse responds, be quick to release the pressure. This quick release, offered as soon as the horse gives the desired response, is crucial to helping the horse learn.

When you are quick to release in response to the horse carrying out the desired task, you are said to have "good timing." The same will be true when you are on his back handling reins. Having good timing while riding can be harder because you are also balancing yourself on a moving horse, and the horse has the distraction of someone on his back. Practicing this skill of good timing via groundwork will give you an advantage once you are in the saddle.

1.12 Rosie easily follows the feel of my soft leading hand, directing her forward. My driving hand is still because it is unneeded.

1.13 This is how longeing should look when the horse is cruising on a short line. This is also the position you will want to be in when you "release the pressure" while in longeing position. I have a soft expression, relaxed body, and soft hands. My leading hand is overhand, and there is slack in every part of the rope. Rosie has a relaxed expression, but more importantly, her inside ear is pointing at me. This tells me that she's paying attention and will see my next cue. Rosie has her body curved slightly around me while maintaining a distance that keeps my rope from either getting tight or touching the ground.

■ Gesture to Go

Whether your horse has been longeing for years, or has only recently learned the basics, he should move out on the line with good energy. But in reality, how much do you have to do to get him to move in the first place, and how hard do you have to work to keep him going? Ideally, all you should have to do is lift a finger to get your horse to go faster—and he should stay at that speed until you inform him that it is time to make a change.

When you are watching horses interact in a field, and one puts his ears back at an approaching horse, you will likely see the approaching horse quickly move away. If he doesn't, you will then see the horse with his ears back look hard at the approaching horse. If that horse still doesn't turn, the first horse will dramatically chase the approaching horse away. Our goal with Gesture to Go is similar to this interaction between horses: you want the horse to move to the next faster gait when you simply raise the pointer finger on your driving hand. If he's halted, we want him to walk. If he is walking, we want him to trot. You can begin teaching this exercise either loose in a round pen or on the longe line.

1 Start with your horse well away from you—you want to be sure you are out of kicking range.

2 Next, consider your body position. In this exercise, your horse will interpret the manner in which you aim your head and shoulders the same way he interprets the position of his herd-mate's head and shoulders. If you want your horse to move forward, square your shoulders to his hip. If your shoulders are squared to any part of the horse in front of his heart (located roughly at the girth), your positioning tells your horse to stop. Begin with your shoulders squared to your horse's hip and your driving hand at your hip level; raise your energy and point your index finger up toward the sky. If your horse doesn't shift into the next higher gait after two seconds, lift your energy even higher and raise your hand with your pointer finger still extended to the sky. If your horse still doesn't shift to the next higher gait within two seconds, summon the energy of a rabid raccoon and "fling it" at the horse's haunches (figs. 1.14 A–C). This could be accomplished by a mighty swing of your excess rope, dramatic whip cracking, or anything else that gets your horse's attention and causes him to move forward. Stay out of kicking range, but don't be afraid to make contact with your horse's heels or haunches with a flick of the end of your rope or the lash on your whip.

1.14 A–C To send Rosie forward, I lift my internal energy and the index finger of my driving hand (A). Soon this will be the only cue needed to move the horse into the next faster gait. Because Rosie does not immediately respond to the cue, I raise my energy and my finger higher (B). I'm feeling buoyant inside my body. Rosie raises her energy marginally, but does not move to the next gait. After waiting two more seconds to give her a chance to respond, I summon the energy of a rabid raccoon (C)! I twirl my rope with intent, get aggressive with my posture, and even jump up and down until Rosie moves forward with energy. When she moves to the next gait, I immediately cease "rabid raccoon mode."

3 Once your horse is energetically moving forward, lower your driving hand and finger immediately. Soften your energy back to your belly. Discontinue driving him forward and allow him to naturally come back to the walk.

4 If he doesn't walk after a couple revolutions, ask him to walk with your voice. Be patient and let him come to a walk without jerking on the line. You just made a really big deal about going faster; if you now make a really big deal about going slower, your horse might not feel like he's ever doing the right thing.

5 Once your horse is settled back to the walk for a revolution, repeat your energy and finger lift again, starting at hip level, and progress as you did before to "rabid raccoon level" (if needed) to get your horse to advance to the next fastest gait. If you have good timing, by the third attempt, most horses will understand the first finger lift as a cue to *go*. From now on, body position and a finger lift will be your new cue to your horse for going faster in your groundwork. At first, he may be a bit worried about the cue, but if you are fair and consistent, he should soon happily respond to the gesture because he understands what it means. If at any point your horse starts to ignore the cue, you must immediately go to back to "rabid raccoon mode."

■ Shoo!

Staying safe around your horse is of utmost importance. While we want our horses to seek our companionship, we don't want them to literally climb in our lap. It is important to practice the skill of sending your horse away from you when you are both calm, so that you will be able to do so in a tense situation. The goal of Shoo! is to get the horse to quickly move sideways a few feet away from you, while you are in longeing position.

Before you attempt the Shoo! exercise, be sure you and your horse feel successful with Moving Together (p. 27), Moving Your Energy (p. 26), and the longeing positions (p. 22), and that you have moved toward developing good timing (p. 31). One important note—if your horse is wary about people or you don't think he would ever bump into you because he is nervous about your existence in general, you should skip this exercise for now. If your horse is already jumping away from you when you simply look at him with too much intention, this is not a necessary exercise at this time.

1 Square your shoulders to the horse, raise your energy, flap your rope, wave your arms, even jump up and down until your horse takes a sideways step away from you (fig. 1.15).

2 If these actions don't move your horse away, add a deliberate, hard expression to your face, and look at your horse with intense eyes. You can even say something loudly, like: "Shoo!"

3 As soon as your horse steps away, immediately lower your energy, take a deep breath, and find calm again. Know that *once might be enough*. If you repeat this exercise too much, it will hinder your ability to draw your horse to you in the future. Therefore, when you and your horse are capable of performing "Shoo!" do not repeat the exercise, unless you have a reason to.

■ Back Up

There are dozens of ways to get your horse to back up. We've already practiced one method (p. 30). When we do this next exercise, we want to think about what the horse will feel on his nose when we ride bitless. The goal is to have the horse respond to the slightest increase of pressure on his nose by stepping backward. (Before you begin, review the leading exercise described on p. 19.)

1.15 In the Shoo! exercise, I square my shoulders to her, lean in, step in, increase my energy, and raise both hands to get Rosie to step sideways away from me. Notice that there is no tension on the rope between my leading hand and the halter, so it is clear to Rosie that she is not supposed to come closer to me.

1 Stand close to your horse's throat, facing his tail. Place your leading hand overhand, and use it to push the rope toward the center of the horse's pectoral muscles.

2 As soon as the horse begins to step back, immediately open your leading hand and drop the rope. If your horse didn't back up right away, you can use your driving hand to flap the excess rope in front of his face.

3 As you repeat this exercise, do your best to add pressure on the rope slowly, to avoid causing him to lift his head, hollow his back, or brace against you. If you pick up slowly and softly on the rope, you can likely avoid this pattern of resistance. If despite your best efforts, your horse still braces against you, try to keep the pressure on until he releases the brace, then immediately drop and slacken your rope (figs. 1.16 A & B). With proper repetitions, the bracing period of backing up will diminish, then extinguish.

1.16 A & B The hand position in Photo A is a *pulling* hand. Rosie easily braces against and ignores my request. People often escalate force to get their horses to back up from this cue, but the biomechanics of this action make it difficult to time the release properly. The hand position in Photo B is a *pushing* hand. Rosie steps back when she feels this cue. It will be easy for her to find the release from pressure when she softens at the poll and takes a step back. Use a pushing hand instead of a pulling hand whenever possible in *all* exercises.

■ Poll Flexions

In the last exercise, we taught the horse to shift his weight backward in response to pressure on top of his nose. In this exercise, the horse will now learn to follow the feel of the sides of the halter to turn his head. The goal is for you to be able to take your horse's head from its neutral position and bring it 90 degrees to either side, using just one finger on the horse's halter.

1 Stand next to your horse's shoulder in longeing position and hook the index finger of your leading hand onto the noseband of his halter (or your bitless bridle, as shown in the photos). Gently place the palm of your driving hand on his neck, right behind his ears (fig. 1.17 A).

2 While keeping your driving hand still against the upper part of the horse's neck, behind the jowl, use your leading hand to gently pull the halter toward the horse's

PART 1: GROUNDWORK | 39

1.17 A & B Poll Flexions can be taught in the halter and reviewed in the bitless bridle of your choice, as shown here. It's a fantastic exercise to do just before mounting, especially for a horse that is new to bitless riding. In Photo A, I have placed my driving hand on Rosie's neck, just behind her jowl, as my leading hand grasps the halter. In keeping with the idea of building softness, my posture is relaxed, and my hands are as open as they can be, while still setting a clear boundary. Over two seconds, I gradually introduce the degree of pressure on the halter that I would like Rosie to respond to.

In Photo B, we can see that Rosie easily gave to the pressure on the side of her nose and brought her head around 90 degrees. In response to my hand placed at the top of her neck, she kept the base of her neck straight. However, Rosie is showing a slight head tilt; notice the bottom of her left ear is lower than the bottom of her right ear. Ideally, the horse keeps his ears level throughout this exercise; we don't want to teach a horse to tilt his head, as that will hinder his progress in becoming round (see p. 118) and could negatively affect his soundness and symmetrical development.

To help correct head tilt in this exercise, experiment with the placement of the hand on the horse's neck. Next time, I will try placing my hand on Rosie's face, under her ear, and behind her eye to see which pivot point teaches her to tilt her head less.

withers. When your horse starts to turn his head, immediately release (fig. 1.17 B). The timing of this release is critical; releasing as soon as he turns his head will make the exercise go faster and smoother the next time.

3 If your horse doesn't turn his head right away, you can pull a little harder, but do not jiggle, vibrate, or otherwise change the cue. You may have to exercise a lot of patience, and be prepared to release as soon as his head turns. If your horse starts moving his feet instead, go ahead and move with him a bit while maintaining the same sideways pressure until he stops.

4 Release the pressure right away when he turns his head. If at first your horse only moves his head an inch or less, you should still release right away. This will let your horse know that he is on the right track. Tomorrow, you might get 2 inches of movement. Usually, it takes time to develop a perfect response. Work at it a little each day

1.18 A & B After learning the Poll Flexion exercise with your finger hooked through the noseband, you can take it one step further by using the reins on your bitless bridle to achieve the movement, as shown in Photo A. The vector of your rein action is crucial. Be sure your rein moves straight back toward where you carry your hands when riding as you ask the horse to move his head in the same way he did during the exercise on the ground.

If you compare Photo B to Photo A, you can see that my leading hand (on the rein that applied pressure) has not moved. This is an excellent example of how a trainer's hand should act. Rosie understands the cue, having previously learned it with my finger through her noseband. When she responded to the pressure and adjusted herself to fit the boundary my body was setting, she experienced a release of pressure. I didn't have to try to have good timing in the release, all I had to do was keep my hand still in space. Notice also there is less head tilt here than in fig. 1.17 B; the bottom of Rosie's ears are level.

and you will eventually get your horse to turn his head 90 degrees with a feather light touch (figs. 1.18 A & B). Note: Take care not to pull your horse's head back to neutral (looking straight ahead). Instead, allow his head to move back to neutral naturally after the release. I like to do several repetitions on one side of the horse before switching to his other side. It is normal for this exercise to be more difficult on one side than the other.

■ Shoulder Yield

Once your horse can follow a feel (see p. 30) from longeing position, try this.

1 Stand face to face with your horse, with about 5 feet between you.

2 See if you can have your horse take a step forward and to the side of you. Ask by extending your leading hand in the direction you wish him to go, and lift your energy.

3 If your horse doesn't readily follow the feel, twirl the rope in your driving hand while looking toward his haunches (fig. 1.19).

> **Squaring Off?**
>
> The way you orient your body to the horse's body is important. When two stallions are getting ready to fight, they approach each other head on, with their shoulders squared. We aren't looking to fight with our horses, so we have to be careful that we don't put ourselves in that confrontational posture. If you want your horse to come toward you, be careful *not* to square your shoulders with his. It is much more inviting if you turn your torso slightly away from him, so your body language doesn't say that you are trying to pick a fight.

1.19 Rohan is reluctant to yield his shoulders to me, so I look hard at his right shoulder so he can feel my intention. I use my right hand to have him follow a feel to my right, and my left hand to drive him by flapping excess rope.

■ Arm Yield

When we get on our horse and ride bitless, it will help if he has a clear idea of what pressure from a rider's leg means. Therefore, we are going to teach him about it (or review it, if your horse is already well trained) from the ground first, using your arm in place of your leg. Our goal is to have your horse move sideways away from pressure on his barrel—where your leg will be when you are mounted. Before trying the Arm Yield exercise, review Shoo! and Poll Flexions (pp. 36 and 39), and continue to practice good timing in your release.

Tall? Try This

If you are sufficiently tall, and your horse is sufficiently short in comparison, you may be able to do this exercise in your bitless bridle by holding both reins above your horse's withers with your leading hand and using your driving hand to perform the Arm Yield.

....

1 Stand close to your horse, in longeing position, and use your leading hand to establish a very light feel on your horse's halter. We don't want to pull on him, but we do want to be positioned so the horse will encounter pressure on his nose if he walks forward, instead of going sideways.

2 Next, use your arm to apply pressure to the horse's side where your lower leg will naturally hang while riding. Orient your arm vertically, so it will feel as much like a leg as possible to your horse (fig. 1.20).

3 Upon feeling this pressure, if your horse moves sideways right away, that is great. Praise him and see if he responds just as well on his other side.

4 However, it is possible that your horse will either walk forward, back up, or push back against you. If he walks forward or backs up, move with him and keep the same amount of pressure on him with your arm. Use your leading hand to stop his forward movement. Wait for him to move sideways away from your arm, then immediately release pressure with both your hands and praise him.

5 If your horse struggles to understand he should move sideways instead of forward when he feels the pressure on his side, it could be helpful to have your horse face a fence, so going forward is no longer a possibility. Going sideways will be the easiest thing for him to do to relieve the pressure of your Arm Yield.

1.20 To perform an Arm Yield, from longeing position, I use my leading hand on Rosie's halter, and my driving arm as a substitute for my leg. As soon as Rosie moves away from my driving arm, I release pressure from both my arms. In this position, all I will have to do is stand still and the pressure will go away as soon as Rosie moves away from me. If your horse hasn't done this exercise before, chances are you will have to move around with him a bit as he tries out moving forward and backward.

6 If instead your horse braces against your arm, or ignores you completely, see if you can inspire some motion with a verbal cue like clucking or kissing. Once he is moving, he will be more likely to move away from arm pressure. If you still don't get a result, concentrate your pressure into your hand over the area where your heel will be. You can make the pressure more intense in this location. Note that subsequent repetitions should always start with mild arm pressure before escalating.

PART 1: GROUNDWORK | 45

Praise the Individual

Praise the horse in a way that makes him feel good. Not every horse likes to be pet or loved on while working. Do you like it when you are trying hard to understand something and every so often someone comes and touches you? Maybe you do, or maybe you think it's obnoxious. You are an individual and so is your horse. If your horse gets nippy or wants to rub on you when you are petting him during praise, try a different form of praise. Some horses feel it is very unfair that you get to pet them, and they don't get to pet you back with their muzzle. If your moments of praise don't feel like they are effective for centering and connecting with your horse, it's worth trying a different reward for him.

You might find your training sessions are more peaceful if you substitute petting with one of the following:

- Verbal praise ("You're so smart!"), while keeping your distance.

- Share a point of view with your horse. Orient your body to match your horse's, and think about what he is seeing and hearing for a few moments. These moments of stillness and calm can revitalize your connection with your horse.

- Ground yourself. While it seems like this one is all about you, when you take some deep breaths, check in with all your body parts, and notice your environment, your horse will likely let go of some tension too.

- "Pet" your horse with your brain waves. Take a moment to pause and genuinely feel gratitude, awe, or joy about what your horse has just done at your request. Your horse will recognize the lightness of your thoughts.

■ Draw to Stop

When you work with your horse, it is important to foster a relationship where he wants to be with you. This exercise teaches your horse that he can approach you when invited, and that groundwork isn't only about skills that push the horse away from the trainer. At the same time, being able to halt your horse at a distance, without touching him, is a fantastic way to set boundaries with your horse via gesture, rather than force.

Before you begin, your horse should be able to Follow a Feel, and you should have control of your energy (pp. 30 and 25).

If your horse has a hard time turning in on the longe line and walking toward you, he is not ready for Draw to Stop. And if you determined your horse should skip the Shoo! exercise (p. 36), you should skip this exercise, too. For these horses, we will pick up the skill again when we Shoulder Yield to change direction (p. 54).

1 Begin by longeing your horse at the walk, making sure his head is pointing in the direction of travel, or slightly inward on the circle. You've already practiced Poll Flexions (p. 39), so you should be able to have some influence on where he looks.

2 Next, pick a point directly behind you and walk backward toward it. Your horse should turn in and walk toward you with a slack rope (fig. 1.21). If he doesn't, check that you aren't aggressive in your posture—make sure your shoulders aren't square to his and that you aren't looking at him with too "hard" an eye. It may even help you to slouch a bit and smile softly. Finally, check in with your hands to make sure they are as relaxed and open as they can be without dropping the rope.

1.21 Rohan comes toward me on a slack line as I walk backward.

PART 1: GROUNDWORK | 47

1.22 Rohan didn't stop right away when I squared my shoulders to him and put my hands in "stop" position, so I step toward him and direct my energy his way.

3 If you are sure that you have inviting body language and your horse still isn't following you back on a subsequent attempt, you can help him turn by taking slack out of the line as you step back.

4 Once your horse has turned his whole body toward you and is coming right at you, keep walking backward for a couple more steps. Then stop your feet, square your shoulders to his, stand tall, and hold both hands up in a "stop" position. Your horse should halt right where he is. Make sure that you ask for this stop when he is still at least 5 feet away from you, or he might have trouble seeing your hand signal. If your horse doesn't stop right away, lift your energy and put a bit of drive into it, like you did with Shoo! (p. 36). For example, you can jump up and down or take an aggressive step toward him (fig. 1.22).

5 Repeat this exercise until you can do it with slack in the rope the whole time.

> **"How Are You, Horse?"**
>
> Once your horse comes to a halt in Draw to a Stop, take some time to dwell there. Keep your distance from him and start to notice what he's feeling. You will start to recognize if he's in a frame of mind where he's capable of learning, versus one where he's just trying to survive what you are doing with him. Notice if he may be expressing tension in his eyes, nostrils, and lips. If you wait a while, you might see him lick and chew. This is a sign he's processing what just happened, so you should pause and allow that processing to continue.
>
> You might notice him yawn, shake his neck, or sigh. All these are signs that he is trying to regulate his emotions and should be praised. Hopefully, you will also see him put his nose to the ground or look away. This behavior is normal when the horse is deciding whether to connect with you or not. If he starts to move away after putting his nose to the ground, he isn't ready to connect yet. If he doesn't move away after putting his nose to the ground, he is trying to connect with you.
>
> If your horse doesn't do any of these things, you need to work on yourself. It is likely he doesn't feel like he is able to connect with you, so work on becoming more mindful. Start with your breathing; be aware of how long you breathe in and out. Feel your body—the sensations in your hands, your toes in your boots, your front side, your back side, and the muscles in your face. Release any tension you find. Feel your feet grounding you. Listen to the sounds around you. Can you hear birds singing, horses eating, people talking? Keep breathing in this moment, feeling your body, listening to the sounds around you, and watching your horse with soft eyes as he starts to release his tension, too.

■ Haunches Yield

As we develop our common language with our horse, we can go from large concepts (moving the entire horse) to smaller concepts (moving half the horse at a time) to refined concepts (moving just one foot at a time). The Haunches Yield is the first exercise we teach the horse that has him moving pairs of his legs in different vectors. In order for a horse to become round and lift his back up, his hind legs need to move farther underneath his body. The Haunches Yield teaches your horse to take big steps with his hind legs, while his front legs remain on the spot.

1 Begin from a halt. Standing in longeing position, softly ask your horse to tip his nose toward you.

2 With your leading hand, push the rope toward the point of your horse's hip. You might need to take the slack out of the line by using your driving hand to pull the

1.23 Alex is using a pushing hand directed at Quincy's hip. Quincy followed the cue from the rope even before the slack came out of the line and responded by abducting (stepping out) his right hind leg.

rope through your leading hand. Watch for the horse to step out with the hind leg farthest from you or cross his hind leg closest to you over his other hind leg (fig. 1.23). Either way, his haunches will move away from you. His front feet should either stay still or step in place.

3 Once you see one of the hind legs moving away from you, release the pressure from the rope and return your leading hand to neutral. Finish in a halt.

■ **Maestro**

Our next exercise is called the Maestro because you need to get in and out of the Haunches Yield position quite quickly. You might feel like your leading hand is moving as fast as an orchestra conductor (or "Maestro") moves his baton. Our goal with this exercise is to teach the horse to step at least one hind foot out of his longeing circle, then continue forward, without slowing down or stopping. Before you begin, review Follow a Feel (p. 30), Gesture to Go (p. 33), Poll Flexions (p. 39), and the Haunches Yield (p. 49).

1 Begin in longeing position, and send your horse out on a circle at the walk. (The Maestro should always be taught at the walk. Once horse and trainer are competent at the walk, it can be performed in the trot.)

2 Next, perform a Haunches Yield by pushing the rope in your leading hand toward his hip (fig. 1.24 A).

3 As soon as you see one of his hind legs move away from you, immediately go back to the Follow a Feel position (fig. 1.24 B). The horse should maintain the walk rhythm and continue in a circle around you without ever stopping his feet.

4 If you are having trouble getting your horse to yield his haunches, stop and practice Poll Flexions and the Haunches Yield instead. Your horse needs to be willing to follow the pressure on the rope as you take the slack out of it.

Engaging vs. Disengaging the Haunches

This exercise looks similar to an exercise referred to by many trainers as "disengaging the haunches." To disengage the haunches, you use a haunches yield to take a horse that is moving and bring him to a stop. While there is definitely a place for this exercise in a horse's training, do not confuse it with what we are doing in this book. The exercises taught here *engage* the haunches. We are putting the haunches in a position to help the horse propel himself forward with a flexion and bend that is appropriate for the line of travel he is on. This engagement of the haunches puts the horse in a position that is biomechanically helpful and allows the trainer to make changes in the horse's carriage.

1.24 A My leading hand is pushing toward Risa's hip as she lifts her inside hind leg off the ground. She has responded by adducting (stepping under) with that leg. The shadow of my hand on her flank is where my eyes are, as well as where I am aiming with my leading hand. I have my driving hand ready to twirl or toss my rope if she needs encouragement to continue her forward movement.

PART 1: GROUNDWORK | 51

1.24 B After Risa responds to my first request to yield her haunches with one step, I immediately move my leading hand forward to encourage her to Follow the Feel and continue moving around me on the circle. My driving arm is also extended, since she needed encouragement to continue moving forward.

5 If you struggle to get your horse to go forward again after the Haunches Yield, you are probably dwelling in the Haunches Yield position too long. Time the movement of your leading hand to match one of the horse's hind legs. Bring your leading hand toward your horse's hip while that leg is airborne, and then bring your leading hand forward again once that leg is in its weight-bearing phase. You may need to gesture to your horse that he needs to go (p. 33) so it is clear that he's supposed to keep moving and not stop.

■ Shoulder Yield in Motion

A Shoulder Yield in Motion builds on the work you did previously with Shoulder Yield and Draw to a Stop (pp. 43 and 46). When completed successfully, a Shoulder Yield in Motion will cause the horse to change direction while longeing, without stopping or changing speed.

1 To begin, from the walk, draw the horse in to you as you did during the Draw to a Stop exercise (p. 46).

52 | SOFT, ROUND, AND BITLESS

2 Keep stepping backward, switch your leading and driving hands on the rope, then perform a Shoulder Yield (p. 43) to get the horse to move in the new direction as you stop your feet. *Do not* step to the side to allow the horse to move around you—that would be a "person-yield." Instead, hold your ground, and have the horse step around you (figs. 1.25 A–C).

3 Send the horse on a circle around you in the new direction.

1.25 A & B Rohan begins to turn in toward me, with slack in the line, as I step back (A). I continue to step back until all four of Rohan's feet are pointed straight at me (B).

1.25 C I switch my leading hand and driving hand, stop my feet, and hold my ground to yield Rohan's shoulders as he moves through the Shoulder Yield to change direction.

Kaboom!

Horses can carry emotional tension in their shoulders. You might notice that your horse tends to "explode" out of the Shoulder Yield in Motion to release this tension. I often use this exercise as one way to decide if a horse is ready to be mounted or if he needs more time—and practice with Shoulder Yields—to focus and settle.

4 If you feel like your horse is getting too close, you need to step backward either longer or faster in order to create more room for the movement. If you feel your horse is pushing his shoulder into you as he passes by, roll your rope (p. 24) toward his shoulders, and be mindful that he moves his haunches away from you.

5 Once you and your horse are doing this exercise well at the walk, try it at the trot. It can help to run forward with your horse for a few steps before running backward. When you are in the "holding your ground" phase, running in place might help to keep your horse's energy up and prevent him from breaking gait.

54 | SOFT, ROUND, AND BITLESS

PUTTING IT ALL TOGETHER FOR SOFT, ROUND GROUNDWORK

DEVELOPING A DIAGNOSTIC EYE

Congratulations—now that you've completed these exercises, you have amassed a solid set of tools to help your horse be the best riding horse he can be, with or without a bit. But what does "the best riding horse your horse can be" look like? What does it feel like?

The best way I know to work through these questions is by doing groundwork on a large circle. When my horse is traveling on a circle, I want to see him moving freely forward and curving his body onto the line of travel. He should have an eye and ear focused on me. His back should be relaxed, and he should be in balance. His neck should be a suitable height; not so low that it puts his weight onto his forehand, and not so high that it hollows his back or shortens his stride.

I want my horse to be able to hold that ideal position with minimal guidance from me. At first, I expect him to come in and out of this ideal posture often, and then less frequently as his body gains strength and flexibility. When your horse is moving on a circle around you, he should be carrying himself in that desirable "round" frame we talked about earlier in this book (see p. 6).

SOFTENING TO THE HAND

The following exercises help establish the ideal position for the horse during groundwork. Once this position is found on the ground, it will be easier to replicate under saddle.

■ Poll Flexion in Motion

In this exercise, you turn your horse's head slightly toward you while longeing. It builds on the skills you developed with Follow a Feel (p. 30), Gesture to Go (p. 33), and Poll Flexions (p. 39).

Side-Reins: Yes or No?

Some equestrians try to create a round frame on the longe line by using side-reins. But side-reins limit the motion of a horse's neck and put him into a relatively static position. His entire body will adjust to the rigidity of the side-reins.

You can get your horse round *without* side-reins, which gives him more freedom and mobility in the base of the neck than doing so with them. You will see him adjust the height of his neck as his muscles fatigue or as his balance changes. Horses in side-reins often cope with balance issues and muscle fatigue by leaning into the bit or developing compensation patterns in their bodies. Without side-reins, he will be able to explore other ways of balancing himself in self-carriage and develop the capability to be soft in the rider's hands.

1 For best success, review the Poll Flexion exercise before sending him away from you out on a circle, and then ask him to flex his poll and bring his nose slightly toward you (figs. 1.26 A & B). Because you reviewed the Poll Flexion at the halt, he will already be thinking about the correct response. Move your leading hand about 10 percent as much as you did during the Maestro exercise (p. 50), though the direction and feel of your hand is otherwise the same.

2 Timing is crucial—as soon as your horse flexes at the poll, release the pressure. If you hold the flexion at the poll too long, you teach your horse to brace against pressure.

3 When your horse is no longer flexing his poll toward you, immediately ask for another flexion. Release, and give the horse the opportunity to carry himself in the correct posture. Avoid the temptation of holding pressure to keep him in the desired position. Instead, you may ask for eight or more flexions on a single circle. This is absolutely okay! When your timing is good, you will start to notice that your horse can go longer without needing the cue to flex his poll.

4 Now that your horse is responding to a cue to flex his poll to the inside, check on the position of his haunches. You want him to be lively with his hind end, stepping his inside hind leg toward the midline of his body. To achieve this, use the Maestro exercise (p. 50).

■ Neck Lowering

Horses naturally carry their heads in different positions, whether due to conformation, breed, or attitude. But when most horses are relaxed, if you draw a horizontal line from the top of the withers toward the head, it should connect somewhere between the bottom of his ears and his eyes. If your horse's head is too high (above this general guideline), it is helpful to figure out if he is high-headed because he

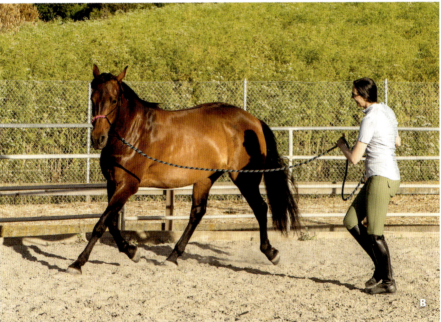

1.26 A & B Rohan's body is bending and poll is flexing *away* from me in A, which is clearly seen due to the fact that his nose is pointing to the *outside* of the longe circle. Every other longeing photo in this book shows a horse with his nose pointing to the *inside* of the circle, bending and flexing *toward* me, as shown in B.

Putting the Tools Together

As your horse goes along, keeping track of his bend and the height of his neck go hand in hand. You will use the Poll Flexion in Motion (p. 55) and Maestro (p. 50) exercises to help get him in the right position, and then ask him to Follow a Feel (p. 30) forward and down. The Gesture to Go exercise (p. 33) will help him go forward without resistance, which allows him to hold his body positioning.

One important note—after you apply any of these tools, you will not see the desired result on the very next step that your horse takes. In fact, for the first day or two you use these tools with your horse, you might not see the desired result at all. As your horse begins to understand the language you are speaking at a distance, you will start to see the changes occur. Typically, when a horse is starting to figure out that lowering his neck feels good, he experiments with lowering his neck about six steps after the trainer releases the cue. The time between the cue and response will lessen with practice.

....

is emotionally stressed, or if that's where his body is accustomed to traveling. Either way, we need to help him relax the muscles over his back and under his neck.

A horse that is high-headed because he is anxious or full of energy needs help to make him feel safe and relatively relaxed before other training can begin. I might let him blow off some steam with a "frolic" at first—ideally, with him free (at liberty), and without being chased around. However, this is sometimes not possible, which is when this exercise comes in handy.

1 Start with the horse moving in a longe circle around you.

2 Check in with your Shoo! exercise (p. 36) to keep yourself safe.

3 Then, add frequent direction changes using the Shoulder Yield in Motion (p. 52). We know that this exercise can release pent up emotions, so if your horse is already on edge, be prepared for some dramatic reactions.

4 The frequent changes of direction serve to focus the horse's mind and attention, as well as supple his body. He

A

58 | SOFT, ROUND, AND BITLESS

will need to free up his shoulders and roll his rib cage as he turns. Once you have the horse's body properly aligned, and his mind sufficiently calm, be sure that he can hold this posture on a loose line. He will be looking to follow your feel in this moment, so let the weight of the rope be all he feels, not a brace from his trainer's hand. He will naturally stretch downward in this moment.

5 At first it will take your horse several strides to begin to stretch his neck down. Allow time for that to happen while maintaining the gait with your energy and gestures. It might not happen the first day you try it.

6 It's likely that your horse will bring his neck down, then bring it back up again. Be ready to refresh his bend, using your flexion or Maestro tools, then release and wait for him to lower his head again. At first you will feel like you are mostly correcting

1.27 A & B Risa's head is a bit higher than I would like (A). She is sensitive to my aids for Maestro (p. 50) at this point, so they are much less pronounced than when she was learning the skill. I ask her to yield her haunches, and she responds by increasing her bend and activating her inside hind leg.

Next, I bring my leading hand back to neutral and use it to ask Risa to follow a slightly downward feel. I relax my shoulders and tell Risa how wonderful she is. In response, Risa lowers her neck and lifts her back (B). This round posture is what many people are after when they use side-reins and bitting rigs. But Risa has never worn side-reins—instead of being forced into this posture, she has learned to follow soft cues to adopt a dynamic and healthy way of traveling.

and not lingering in the neck lowered position. With practice, the neck lowered position will become easier and you won't have to correct your horse's carriage as often (figs. 1.27 A & B).

■ Rainbow

In this exercise, you will ask the horse to move in a semicircle back and forth before you, without changing speeds. It is most useful for horses that consistently accelerate when changing direction—skip it if your horse is feeling sluggish. If your horse tends to "blow by" you, instead of responding to poll flexion cues and drawing in, Rainbow can help with that, too. Before you begin, review Follow a Feel (p. 30), Shoulder Yield (p. 43), and Shoulder Yield in Motion (p. 52).

1.28 Rohan dramatically accelerates as my leading hand helps him turn at the end of the Rainbow. Since I have the arena fence to stop him, I don't have to expend energy to limit his movement. I can remain soft, with my energy "down" for as long as it takes for him to match it. Eventually, he will realize that my energy feels good and decide to mirror it through the turns.

1 To get started, find a fence or wall that your horse will not jump. Stand with your back to the fence and move your horse toward it in an arc in front of you, at a distance.

2 Each time your horse gets to the end of the arc (where he meets the fence) ask him to change direction in motion (Shoulder Yield in Motion) and travel the arc in the opposite direction. He should become steadier in his speed when he realizes he's going to have to stop for the wall in a few strides. Boundaries are comforting to your horse, and he will begin to relax into the limits you've put on his direction and speed (fig. 1.28).

3 Once your horse is on board with going the speed and direction you choose, check in that he is also bending appropriately around you. When viewed from above, your horse should appear to be a little "shorter" on the side closer to you, and a little "longer" on the side farther away. The curve of his body will match the curve of the arc. If he is not curved in your direction, ask for a series of Poll Flexions (p. 39).

Round and Round

Circles are the best shape to teach a horse to be round through his body. An even arc of travel on the circle leads to consistent bend, which will then lead to a round topline. However, performing endless circles is not ideal for a horse's body. I rarely do this type of work with a horse for longer than eight minutes in a session, changing direction often during that time. Bigger circles are easier on a horse's joints, but it is harder to influence a horse from a greater distance. Keep this in mind during your training sessions.

■ Raising the Withers

When your horse's head is too low, he might be dumping his weight onto his forehand. This isn't a healthy posture, as it puts extra strain on his front legs. We will now combine two skills you have already mastered—the Energy exercise (p. 26) and Maestro (p. 50)—to teach your horse to elevate his withers while simultaneously lowering his haunches. This time, Maestro will be followed by Follow a Feel (p. 30) inward and upward, and a "lifting" of your energy.

To help raise a horse's head, ask him for Maestro (see p. 50) and accentuate *going forward* at the end of the exercise. Imagine there is a rigid pole resting on the front of your horse's hind hoof and connecting to your horse's chin. When your horse brings his hind foot more underneath his body, it will push his chin up. It is important that the neck comes up due to the engagement of the horse's thoracic sling muscles (responsible for suspending the horse's torso between his forelimbs),

1.29 In this moment, Risa is coming out of a Maestro, seen by the swing of her inside hind leg under her body. Since I am looking for a more uphill frame, I have straightened my posture and raised my energy level. I am also carrying my leading hand about level with where I want the corner of her mouth to be.

not because he braces the underside of his neck. Engaging the thoracic sling muscles will create a lift in the withers and aid in lowering the haunches (fig. 1.29).

A horses that travels on his forehand with his neck too low is essentially slouching. Help your horse find self-carriage with his neck up by making sure *you* are not slouching! Hold your body a bit straighter and carry your hand higher as you ask your horse to carry his forehand higher. As you develop language and connection with your horse, he will try to mirror your energy and posture.

1 Use Maestro (p. 50) to bring your horse's inside hind leg under his body.

2 As soon as the inside hind leg steps under his body, drive the horse forward while bringing your leading hand higher than the knot connecting the rope and halter.

3 Maintain your upright posture, hand position, and driving energy to continue helping the horse move forward in this uphill frame. As your horse is able to hold this frame for longer, try to do less with your hands to encourage the frame.

4 When the horse loses balance and leans forward, repeat the exercise from Step 1.

BALANCE

When the horse carries his neck at the ideal height, in addition to developing the muscles he needs to carry himself in a round frame, he is also positively affecting his *longitudinal balance*. Horses generally carry 60 percent of their weight on their forelegs; however, especially with a rider on board, it is healthier for them to carry more weight on their hind legs. When they are encouraged to move in a round frame, we are changing the horse's weight distribution between his front and hind legs.

> **Balance Maintenance**
>
> Maintaining effortless balance is not something that you can "set and forget." Once balance is achieved, horse and rider need to be able to quickly notice and correct balance deficits to maintain it. Those horses and riders who have the best balance are usually the quickest at making these corrections.

We also must consider our horse's *lateral balance*, meaning the weight distribution between his right and left legs. Ideally, your horse should be traveling with 50 percent of his weight on the left legs, and 50 percent of his weight on his right legs. However, it is fairly common for horses to have uneven weight distribution when working with people. Without equal weight distribution,

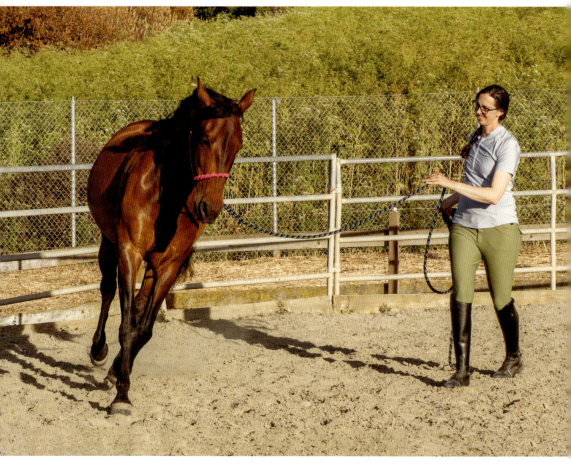

1.30 There are lots of nice things about this photo. Risa and I are communicating well, we both have soft expressions, and we are softly holding our respective ends of the rope. She has good longitudinal balance, with her poll raised above her withers and without bracing on the underside of her neck. However, although Risa is nicely bent around me on the circle, we can see that she is leaning in, a sign she has lost lateral balance.

The circle is very small, which makes the leaning in more noticeable. Looking at where Risa's front feet are placed, we can see that she isn't putting her front hooves directly under their respective shoulders. Her outside front foot is coming down close to the midline of her body, but more importantly, her inside front foot was placed at or beyond the midline of her body. It is this inside foot that needs to change its trajectory.

To have a more level lateral balance, Risa's inside front foot needs to abduct (step away from her body). This will make her back level from side to side. Some people can access the horse's front foot and bring it toward them via their groundwork, which makes the most sense to the horse, but this is difficult to achieve. Other trainers opt to focus on pushing the horse's ribcage away from them, which often levers the inside front foot more toward the inside of the circle and away from the horse's midline.

64 | SOFT, ROUND, AND BITLESS

your horse lacks a sense of safety and does not feel good about giving influence of his posture up to a human.

Does your horse struggle to get one of his canter leads? Is there a direction that is more difficult for him to bend, or a way he can't move sideways as easily? All of these issues may be the result of poor lateral balance.

The two most common examples of lateral balance loss in the horse are "falling in" on a circle, or the opposite, "popping a shoulder out." Many times, when a horse falls in around a turn, people try to solve the problem by using more inside leg to push him out. When the horse instead pops his shoulder out, they try to solve the problem by pushing with the outside leg or rein. But addressing these issues in this way is akin to playing "whack-a-mole." As soon as you fix the leaning in, the horse starts to pop his shoulder out. It is better to solve the root issue instead.

A horse showing either of these common lateral balance issues likely is landing with too much weight on his inside front foot. That's right—both these issues stem from the same root problem. We need to help the horse abduct his inside front leg, meaning more easily move the limb out and away from his body (fig. 1.30). It may seem counterintuitive, but to keep a horse from falling in to the right on a circle, we need to move his right front leg more to the right. He is falling in because he doesn't have an adequate base of support, and he doesn't feel balanced. So, let's help him find his balance!

> ### Abduct vs. Adduct
>
> *Abducting* a leg is moving that leg *away* from the horse's body. It might help to associate "abduction" with a child being abducted that is taken *away* from her family.
>
> *Adducting* is bringing the leg *inward*. Just like *adding* cookies to a pile is bringing them *in* toward the rest of the cookies.

■ Range of Motion (ROM)

Here's an exercise to help make sure your horse is equally adept at abducting and adducting all four legs, independently. You'll be using both your Shoulder Yield (p. 43) and Haunches Yield (p. 49) to help improve his range of motion. The good news is that you can increase your horse's flexibility to build symmetry. Work on it a little bit every day; don't expect to cure his restriction in one session. That would be the same as thinking you could do the splits after only one day of stretching.

Exiting or Entering Stress?

Horses often make the same facial expressions when they are *becoming* stressed as they do when their stress is *declining*. We often think of a horse yawning, or licking and chewing, as being relaxed. But evidence shows that a horse displaying these signals might be coming *out of* a stressful situation…or he might be coming *into* a stressful situation. As your horse's trainer, it is your duty to pay attention to these calming signals and use context clues as to whether your horse is becoming more tense or more relaxed. This is crucial, since it is very difficult for anyone, human or horse, to learn while feeling anxious.

1 Start by checking on the lateral range of motion in each of your horse's legs. Use the Haunches Yield to check on hind leg mobility. As your horse performs the exercise, does he *abduct* his outside leg (moving it away from his body) and *adduct* his inside (moving it toward his body)? Does he have the same range of motion when you switch sides and ask for a Haunches Yield in the other direction? Watch your horse in motion and notice where he puts his feet in relation to the centerline of his body. On a circle, you want your horse's inside hind leg to step closer to his midline; this is part of the mechanics of how a horse bends on a curve. However, you don't want him to step so far under his body that his hind leg crosses his midline and impedes the outside hind leg from swinging forward. Check to see if he travels with the same asymmetries when you change direction.

2 Use the Shoulder Yield to check his front leg mobility, and consider the same questions.

3 Chances are that you noticed your horse has at least one restriction of movement. Your horse likely won't feel good about traveling in a round frame in self-carriage until he has adequate lateral balance. You have been developing a language with your horse through your groundwork, and you can use that language to influence a singular foot. Go slow and pay attention to where the horse is shifting his weight. Identify one leg that you want to abduct or adduct. When you want the leg to move away from you, use your *yielding* tools as that leg is coming off the ground. When you want the leg to move toward you, time the *draw* on your rope.

MAGIC IN THE STILLNESS

Wouldn't it be great if you could apply a tool to a horse and get results right away? Sometimes it works like that, and other times it doesn't. Unfortunately, the desire for instant results means sometimes humans simply go too fast for the horse. We need to remember that while we may have a clear picture of what we want the horse to do in our head, the horse simply does not have that same picture. He has to guess what it is that you want, and he wants to guess right. But when he does guess right, often, humans rush him on to the next thing right away. Unfortunately, this can leave your horse bewildered as to which of his responses was actually desired. This in turn can impede retention of the training.

Whether teaching a horse a new skill, or reviewing an existing skill, when he makes a response that is closer to correct than the last one, give him several moments to solidify that response in his brain before asking again (see Praise the Individual, p. 46).

When we are working to help a horse relax, we need to be even more patient. As humans, we tend to want to *DO* things to solve a problem. Direction changes, yields, and flexions are all great tools, but without building in the time for *stillness*, it is no different than someone telling you, "Relax!" 15 times in quick succession.

As your horse is starting to relax and connect with you, even if it is just a small try, give a release and wait for him to regulate his own emotions. When a horse is coming out of a stressful situation, it's important to wait for him to give you some signs (what Rachaël Draaisma calls "calming signals" in her book *Language Signs and Calming Signals in Horses*) that he is ready to learn again. If you see him licking and chewing, you are on the right track but need to wait a bit longer for your horse to relax his eyes, nose, and mouth (see Draw to a Stop on p. 46). You might get an audible sign that he is ready to learn again if he blows out through his nose or takes a deeper breath. Experiment with waiting longer and see if your horse gets even more relaxed than you thought was possible. You might be surprised to see that your horse actually had more emotions to process—and ability to self-regulate—than you thought.

PART 2

EXPLORING BITLESS BRIDLES

UNDERSTANDING YOUR EQUIPMENT

Now that you have completed the exercises in Part 1, you and your horse have developed a language that can be translated from the halter and lead rope to the bitless bridle and reins. But with all the options for bitless bridles out there, which one is best for you and your horse?

BITLESS BRIDLE PARTS AND HOW THEY FIT

It is possible for a bridle to cause pain, whether it has a bit or not. When choosing a bridle, avoid headstalls that target the weak and sensitive areas of a horse's head, such as the poll and lower nose. When I choose a bitless bridle, I always feel the material of the bridle where it will be touching the horse. Is it soft and smooth? Is there rough stitching that can be felt by your horse?

I was taught to assess the "pinchiness" of a snaffle bit by draping the joint over the web of my thumb and seeing if it pinched my skin when I manipulated the rings. I still perform this test on every bit before I select it. The Mellor Pen Test is another method used to help people empathize with the physical sensations of wearing a bit. In this test, humans use a ballpoint pen to apply pressure to their lips and gums in order to relate to a horse's experience of wearing a bit.

I created a similar physical test for a bitless bridle: to evaluate the sensation a horse might experience with a bitless bridle, wear the noseband as a crown. (You will absolutely look silly doing this, so maybe check to see who is watching first.) Since practicing this technique, I've discovered that nosebands I thought were gentle were actually aversive and abrasive against my skin (fig. 2.1).

To feel the effects of each of the other parts of your bitless bridle, enlist the help of a friend. One of you will hold the bridle from the crownpiece, and the other will use her hands to fill up the space the horse's nose will occupy (fig. 2.2). The person holding the crownpiece should activate the bridle by pulling on the reins at the angle they will be used when someone is in the saddle. While doing this, consider the following questions.

- What is the lightest pressure that can be felt by the "horse" when the reins are activated?

- Where is pressure felt? The front of the nose? Under the jaw? At the poll?

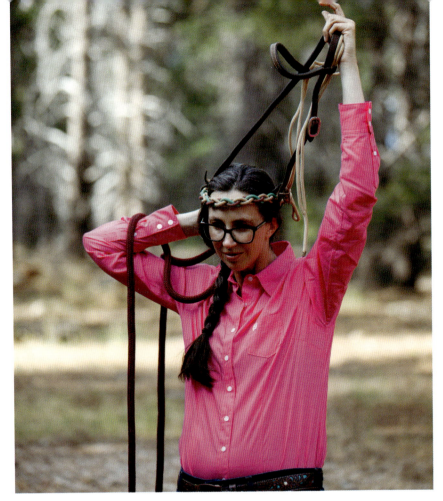

2.1 This loping hackamore was not a comfortable crown. Assessing it on my own body gave me increased awareness of how my horses might feel when they wear it.

- Does the quality of the pressure change if only one rein is activated?

- What changes if the "rider's" hands are elevated?

- How does it feel when her hands are lowered?

- What if her hands are close together? Far apart?

ANATOMY AND FIT

There are some bitless bridles that are uncomfortable for the horse to wear, even if there is no pressure at all on the reins. You must keep in mind where the weak and sensitive spots are located on the horse's head. Avoid pressure on these areas to

2.2 We are actively practicing our empathy by testing out this mechanical hackamore. Ruby and I want to see what our horses will feel when we ride them with it.

help keep your horses happy and healthy, and pay attention to how the headstall is adjusted in the following areas.

Nose and Jaw

The most basic consideration is the height of the noseband. If you slide your hand down the front of your horse's face, you will notice a spot where the texture softens. This is the end of the nasal bone and the beginning of nasal cartilage. Make sure your noseband sits on the bone, *not* the cartilage. Improperly fit or tight nosebands can cause bone thinning, remodeling, nerve damage, and vascular damage (fig. 2.3). When your noseband is adjusted too low, it can also restrict your horse's breathing. Be careful that your noseband isn't too high either, or you might run into a cluster of nerves. The noseband should sit a little more than an inch below the lower end of the horse's cheek bone.

While the "ideal" tightness of the noseband can vary, a good place to start in checking the adjustment is to place your thumb between the noseband and the lower jaw. You should be able to get your thumb in there easily, feeling the hairs on your horse's lower jaw on one side of your thumb, and the noseband on the other side of your thumb, without any pinching.

When the noseband is adjusted too tight, it might be difficult for

2.3 This horse has scarring from a noseband that was fitted too low on his face. You can not only see where the skin has been broken but also the remodeling of the nasal bone and cartilage from extended use with the noseband in an incorrect position. I suspect that the offending noseband was a *serreta*, a noseband with metal teeth; however, I have seen similar remodeling even from improperly fitted sidepulls, which are generally considered a mild option.

2.4 Here are four sidepull noseband options, all of which attach to a regular bridle. From left to right: The black noseband with blue padding is flat, wide, and very heavy due to the hardware and the number of stabilizing straps. It has a mild effect and is very stable on the horse's head. It's great for a horse that likes clear signals and doesn't mind a bit of extra weight. The next three options are attachments that fit directly onto the headstall you already have in place of a bit. (You won't have the stablizing effect of the first sidepull bridle with its additional straps.)

The corded blue noseband has a corrugated texture that the horse will feel as the reins slide the noseband across his face. Paired with a curb strap and headstall, this noseband has more texture than the leather ones. The brown flat and wide noseband is made with very light materials. It has a similar feel to the first sidepull, but is preferred by horses who value lightweight equipment over stability. The brown jumping cavesson feels like a rounded nylon rope covered with leather and is the type of noseband I used in conjunction with a bit with Shotgun Jack (p. 3). It feels sharper to the horse than the other options pictured here.

your horse to distinguish between a sensation on his face that is meant to be a cue, versus the pressure of the noseband when it is in neutral. Tight nosebands stress horses. On the other hand, if the noseband is too loose, it might twist and pull the cheekpiece into the horse's eye. A loose noseband could also cause a loss of refinement in the communication from the rider. Note that some bridles are designed with modifications that allow the noseband to be more stable when adjusted more loosely.

Ears and Poll

The crownpiece is the part of the bridle that goes behind the horse's ears and sits over the poll. Be sure it isn't sitting right on top of, or squeezing at, the sensitive base of the horse's ears. A longer browband or a cut back crownpiece can help alleviate this problem.

Check to see if there is a pressure point on your horse's poll. Some horses have peaked polls that cause the crownpiece to focus pressure on a small point at the poll's apex. For these horses, consider a crownpiece that allows for poll relief or perhaps modifying your bridle yourself.

MATERIAL: TEXTURE, THICKNESS, AND SHAPE

Feel the material of your bridle where it contacts your horse. Are there any rough spots in the leather or stitching? Is the bridle assembled with even, heavy-duty stitching, or is it held in place with rivets or screws that might pop or rub when the bridle is in use?

A mild noseband will be smooth and soft on the surface where it touches the horse's skin. It will follow the contours of the horse's face. If the noseband is rigid, does it follow the contours of the horse's nose, or does it create high pressure points? Are there open rings or moving parts that could pinch his skin? When it comes to nosebands, we must consider the formula of $P=F/A$: *pressure equals force over area*. What this means is your horse will feel more pressure when you decrease the area that the noseband touches. Nosebands get more severe as they become harder, thinner, heavier, rounder, and rougher.

Your reins and how they connect to your bridle matter. If you've been doing your groundwork without a snap on your lead rope, the feel you get from reins that attach with buckles or ties is going to be more familiar than reins attached with a snap. Check to see if they are made of a natural or synthetic fiber, and if they stretch when under pressure. Stretchy reins muddle the signal of pressure and release.

If you are using loop reins, make sure they aren't so long that the bight (excess loop) dangles where your foot might get stuck in it. They also shouldn't be so short that you can't reach them if your horse puts his head down to graze. For split reins, you might want reins that are weighted with thicker leather at the end farthest from the horse's face. The extra weight reduces the motion of the excess rein. (Make sure your splits aren't so long that your horse steps on them!)

Rein thickness and shape are important too. In general, you don't want a rein that is thicker than the lead rope you use. Thicker reins can be easier for arthritic or injured hands to hold. Thinner reins can be more comfortable for smaller hands, but they can also dig into a rider's fingers when used. Shape and texture is a personal preference. Some like a rounded rein, like a rope. Others like a flat rein that may or may not have a texture to it.

When using flat reins, it is important that they are not twisted between the horse's head and the rider's hands. This direct line provides a clearer signal to the horse. Some flat reins are smooth leather, which is the easiest to shorten and lengthen, but can take more effort to hold at a consistent even length. They can be slippery to hold on to in wet conditions, and rigid if they are poor quality leather or dry. Some riders enjoy woven, braided, rubberized, or padded reins, or those with hand stops.

MOVEMENT

Once you understand how the bitless bridle you are considering feels to your horse and have it fitted to his head correctly (see p. 73 for noseband adjustment, and note your bridle should also have a throatlatch just tight enough that it can't slip over the jowl or a jowl strap that should should be snug, and the attachment point of your bitless bridle should be low enough so that the cheek pieces don't twist into your horse's eyes), see if it moves when in action. If you use one rein, does the bridle twist into the horse's eye on the opposite side? When you activate the rein, does it cause pinching of the horse's skin or pull his hair? When your horse is in motion, does the crownpiece slide too far back? Does the noseband slip lower on his face and rest on his cartilage instead of his nasal bone? Make adjustments to your equipment so that it is not creating its own movement and instead is in a stationary position on the horse's head without causing him pain. If you have a bridle that has moving pieces—like a cross-under, scawbrig, mechanical hackamore, or traditional hackamore—you want to make sure that your bridle doesn't move into a position that pinches your horse, slides the noseband below the nasal bone, or pushes the cheekpiece into his eye.

WEIGHT

There are some bitless bridles that only weigh a few ounces; others are quite heavy. Your horse may have a preference as to what weight is most comfortable for him. If he is already light to the aids, he will likely be happiest in at lightweight bridle.. But if he is greener and wants a clearer signal, a heavy bridle might be more stable on his head and deliver a clearer cue.

LEVERAGE

When we are choosing a bitless bridle, it's important to understand the mechanics that make your equipment function. Many bitless options work solely off nose pressure. Some have elements of constriction. Other bitless bridles work off pressure on the poll and lower jaw.

Consider the point where the cheekpieces of the bridle attach to the noseband. The distance between the point of cheekpiece attachment to the headstall and the place the rein attaches to the noseband can affect the overall stability of the bridle on the horse's head. It can also allow for some movement on the horse's face (sometimes called "pre-signal"), which allows for a different (some may say more "nuanced") quality of pressure than pulling on the nose.

If the bitless bridle has a shank in addition to the noseband, there is an element of leverage that acts on the horse's poll and lower jaw (mandibles). Slip a finger or two between the horse's chin and the curb strap and activate the rein. The pressure you feel on your finger is what your horse feels on his face. Now do the same on the top of your horse's nose. Finally, slip your fingers between the headstall and the poll, and feel how the pressure changes when the rein is activated. Try moving the rein in different directions, and notice how the pressure points can change, whether due to a high hand, low hand, opening rein, or any other way in which you commonly use your reins.

TYPES OF BITLESS BRIDLES

TRADITIONAL HACKAMORE

Good For: Refined Communication
Not Ideal For: English Aesthetic

The traditional Western hackamore is my favorite bitless bridle. It is what I have studied the most, and a great place to start in your bitless journey. At a minimum, it consists of a *bosal* (rigid noseband), a *hanger* (strap that connects both sides of the bosal by traveling behind the horse's ears and over the poll), and a *mecate* (long rope that forms the reins and lead rope—fig. 2.5).

This style of hackamore has a long and rich history, especially with the *vaquero* horsemen of the American West. The materials used to create the traditional hackamore are what the *vaqueros* had on hand as they were working with horses and cattle. All hackamores are not created equal, and you get what you pay for. Poor quality hackamores are poor quality equipment.

The Bosal

The *bosal* (bo-ZAHL) is the noseband section of the hackamore. It traditionally has a rawhide core and added material braided around the core (fig. 2.6). From roughest to softest, this material could be rawhide, latigo, or kangaroo leather.

The bosal has a large knot at the bottom, called the *heel knot*. Smaller knots, called *side buttons*, serve to hold the *hanger* (the strap that goes over the horse's head) in place.

The bosal should fit your horse like a hat, touching all around the horse's nose with even pressure. There should not be gaps of air between the bosal and the horse, except directly under the horse's jaw. There shouldn't be any parts that are particularly tight on the horse's nose either. Achieving this fit may require some after-market shaping (fig. 2.7). To get a bosal to fit a horse better, I usually try to

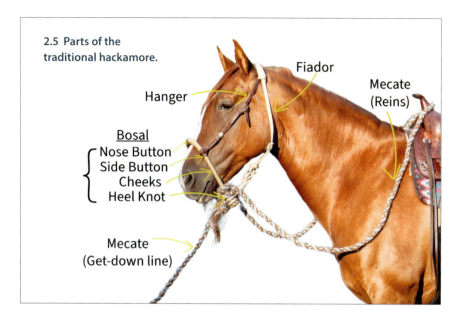

2.5 Parts of the traditional hackamore.

2.6 On the bottom right is a 5/8-inch rawhide bosal. The weight, thickness, and rigidity of the 5/8-inch rawhide hackamore make it the ideal starting place in your hackamore journey. Above the rawhide bosal is a 5/8-inch bosal made of latigo leather. Latigo leather is more pliable than rawhide, which some horses and trainers prefer. Next is a 1/2-inch bosal, which is appropriate for horses that are doing well in the 5/8-inch and ready to go to a lighter piece of equipment. Finally, on top is a kangaroo 3/8-inch *bosalita*. The kangaroo leather is flexible and has a tacky quality. This is suitable for use in a two-rein set up, or under a bitted bridle.

2.7 Rosie's bosal is not a perfect fit. There are air gaps between her face and the nose button (the thick stiff wrapper over the nose). With use, it will start to fit her better. I could hurry the process along by using a shaping device between uses. As it is, she is happy to work in it and it is not causing any rubs, so I will likely take the approach of using it until it fits better.

shape it with my hands before I put it on my horse's head. Usually, this requires squeezing it together at the top and "opening" it at the bottom. When storing a bosal that needs shaping, I wedge something large and hard, like a block of smooth wood, or a wine bottle, in the area that needs to widen. I then use string to tie up the part that needs to become tighter.

You may notice that the side buttons make the hanger pass very close to your horse's eyes. Ideally, you want the hanger to pass as close to the eyes as possible without touching them or injuring the delicate skin nearby. This adjustment allows a greater length between the hanger and the rein, which creates improved signal capacity. Additionally, the bosal's cheeks will have sufficient contact with the sides of his lower jaw to create a "presignal" from the reins; this occurs before the rein fully engages, putting pressure on the horse's nose.

When starting off in the hackamore, choose a bosal that is 3/4- or 5/8-inch in diameter. The extra surface area makes the cues of the thicker bosal easier for the green horse to distinguish. The heavier weight of the heel knot on a thicker bosal also aids in the clarity of signal.

If your goal is to create a Californio-style bridle horse (see sidebar), you will need to introduce gradually thinner bosals before you transition to a bit. But for most people, a 5/8-inch hackamore will serve you well.

> ### From Hackamore to Bit
>
> A Californio-style bridle horse can effortlessly work cattle with invisible cues from his rider. He is said to be "finished" when he can do this while wearing a spade bit (a highly complex curb bit). However, adding a bit happens as one of the last stages in the careful training of these horses. A horse trained in these traditional methods will start off in a 5/8-inch or larger diameter bosal. Once he is solid in that hackamore, he will go to a 1/2-inch bosal. After he is working well in this smaller bosal, his trainer will reduce the diameter of his bosal again, to 3/8-inch and add the spade bit. Initially, there will be a rein on the bosal, and a rein on the spade. The horse will go in this two-rein setup as his rider transitions hackamore cues to bit cues. Finally, the hackamore comes off, and the horse will be "straight up in the bridle."

When sizing the opening of the bosal, you want to make sure it is big enough to accommodate your mecate, but not so big that you need to wrap your mecate more than three times around the bosal to obtain the proper fit (I will explain this in more detail beginning on p. 84). Once your mecate is tied on, put your thumb between the bottom of your horse's jaw and the top of the mecate knot. As already mentioned, when your bosal is properly fitted, your thumb should be contacting the mecate and the hair under your horse's jaw at the same time (fig. 2.8). If you do this size check and find the bosal is too loose or too tight, adjust the number of wraps until you get the proper fit, or find a better-fitting bosal.

2.8 Risa's bosal fits her like a hat. It makes even contact over her nose and along her cheeks. She has an ideal amount of space between the mecate and her lower jaw.

2.9 Match the diameter of your mecate to the diameter of your bosal. In this photo, we have mecates of varying widths and materials. From left to right, a red wool 5/8-inch, turquoise-and-brown mane hair 5/8-inch, pink cotton 5/8-inch, maroon yacht rope 5/8-inch, white-and-brown mane hair 1/2-inch, black-and-brown mane hair 3/8-inch, brown nylon 3/8-inch, and white-and-turquoise cotton 1/4-inch.

The Mecate

The *mecate* (muh-cah-TAY, sometimes called "McCarty") is a rope about 22 feet in length with a diameter that matches the diameter of the bosal. This rope is tied in a certain way (see p. 84) around the bosal to form reins and a "get-down line" (lead rope). The get-down line is used when the rider is unmounted. The reins stay on the horse's neck.

Mecates can be made of horse mane hair, cotton, wool, mohair, nylon rope, and even human hair (fig. 2.9). Hair mecates are the most traditional and have a prickly texture that can act as a sensory aid to help teach the horse to neck-rein. The prickly texture can also help a rider who has hard hands learn to lighten up. Some cotton and mohair mecates are soft in the hand but stretch when in use. If you are working in wet weather, you might prefer a wool or yacht rope mecate.

Mecate Management

When leading with a mecate, the reins will stay over the horse's neck, near the saddle. Your get down line is your lead rope. Keep hold of the get down line until

Tying Your Mecate

1. Hold up the hackamore and locate where the horse's nose will be.
2. Push the tassel end of the mecate through the bottom of the bosal, just above the heel knot (fig. 2.10 A). Most of the time, the tassel is pointing forward toward the horse's lips.
3. This step is important for adjusting the fit of your bosal. Tightly wrap the mecate one to three times around the outside of the bosal, just above the tassel (fig. 2.10 B). Adjust the number of wraps until the bosal is snug.

mounted on the horse. Once mounted, you will need to manage the length of the get down line so it is long enough for the horse to turn his head, but not so long he can snag his foot.

The following are my favorite three ways to manage my excess get down line with safety and comfort in mind:

Method 1: Make a loop with the end of the get down line and pass it through your belt. A heavy loop should stay put and make it easy for you to transition from riding to leading. Never tie it on to your belt.

4. Make reins and adjust them to the proper length by pulling a loop of the mecate through the bosal from the muzzle side and toward the neck. I like a 12-foot loop, and have a 6-foot wingspan, so to measure my rein length, I hold the heel knot with one hand, and the reins with the other (figs. 2.10 C & D).
5. Make a half hitch in your remaining mecate and slide it over the top of the bosal until it rests right on top of the reins (figs. 2.10 E & F).
6. You should end up with the long tail of your mecate coming out the nose-side of the bosal. This is your "get down line" (fig. 2.10 G).

Make sure everything is tight, and the top of your knot is flat where it will contact the horse's lower jaw.

Method 2: Run a loop of the get down line through the gullet of the saddle and over the saddle horn. Do not tie your get down line to the saddle horn; it should pull free if it gets caught on something. This method should only be used if the get down line is short enough that it doesn't dangle below the horse's knee.

Method 3: Tie the get down line to the saddle strings (fig. 2.11):

1 Wind the excess get down line into even coils. Small coils are less likely to hang up a rider during a fall.

2 Flip the coils so the get down line travels from the bosal to the back of the saddle strings.

3 Place the coils so that one of your saddle strings will go over the top of them, and the other will go through them.

4 Take the top string and wrap it twice around the coils.

5 Make a loop with the top string close to the coils.

6 Make two half-hitch knots with the bottom string around the loop of the top string.

7 Pull tight. Tuck the long string through the coils. You now have a quick release knot that should stay put as the horse travels. In the unlikely event the mecate gets hung up on something, the saddle strings will break before causing much damage to you, your horse, or your tack.

Fiador

The *fiador* (rhymes with "Theodore") is an optional piece that makes a hackamore look a bit more like a halter (fig. 2.12). It loops over the heel knot of the bosal, then splits to go behind the horse's ears before being tied back together like a rope halter. It is attached to the hanger with a browband, crown channel, or simple loop.

There are two reasons you may choose to add the fiador. The most important is that a fiador makes your hackamore trail-worthy. If you are leading your horse in his bosal without a fiador and he goes to pull away from you, he is likely to slip out of

2.11 My mecate coils tied to my saddle strings.

2.12 Rosie is soft and round in her hackamore with a fiador.

his hackamore and free himself. This could put you in a tough spot if you are far from home!

The second reason to use a fiador is to hold the bosal steady on the horse's face. This makes it easier for the horse to figure out if a feeling is caused by a signal from the rider versus gravity moving the bosal as the horse moves. Some people like riding with a fiador, and some don't. Fiadors can be inexpensive, so try one out and see if you and your horse like the feel.

Use

You can use a traditional hackamore with one hand or two hands. The goal with any hackamore (and any good riding) is for the rider to principally use her seat and legs to direct the horse, instead of pulling the horse around by his head. The rigidity and fit of the hackamore helps this process. When shaping the horse's body, the rider can position the hackamore where she wants the horse's head to be. Once the horse moves his head to the desired location, the hackamore makes even contact around his nose again.

MECHANICAL HACKAMORE

Good For: Stronger Leverage
Not Ideal For: Subtle Communication

There are many different models of *mechanical hackamores*. English mechanical hackamores; Western mechanical hackamores; variations including *wheel, flower,* and *seahorse*; and even more are being dreamed into existence all the time. All of them consist of a piece that goes over the horse's nose, a curb strap that goes under the horse's jaw, and shanks extending from the junction of these two pieces on either side of the horse's face (figs. 2.13–2.18). They can be used in conjunction with a bit (see p. 93).

Nose Piece

The nose piece goes over the top of the horse's nose. The wider the surface area of the nose piece, the less pressure it applies; therefore, a nose piece that is wide is the gentlest. Often, these gentle nose pieces are made from a thick piece of leather, typically padded with fleece or a synthetic material. More severe nose pieces are thinner and made out of nylon rope or bicycle chain covered with rubber.

2.13 Parts of the mechanical hackamore.

Curb Strap

The part that goes under the horse's lower jaw is called the *curb strap*, based on the similarity of location and function to that of a curb strap on a bit. This strap is where the bulk of effect adjustments come from. The mildest curb straps are made of wide leather; chain curb straps are more severe, and a rigid metal bar delivers the most intense pressure.

Shanks

The style of the shanks and their effect vary significantly. Longer shanks are often believed to be more severe than shorter shanks; however, there is more nuance to consider than length of shank alone when determining its effect on the horse. A longer shank has a longer path from where it hangs without rein pressure, to the point where its movement is stopped by the curb strap. This means a longer shank will have more range of signal than a shorter shank.

    A longer lever can produce a greater force, so a longer shank is capable of being more severe than a shorter shank. However, a longer shank requires the rider to move her hands more before it becomes fully engaged, so in reality, it might be more forgiving than a shorter-shanked hackamore. A rider who lacks the ability to steady her

2.14 Quincy is in a *flower hackamore*, with the reins set on the point offering the highest amount of leverage. The multitude of rings on a flower hackamore allow for the fit to be semi-customizable. You can attach your headstall, noseband, and curb strap on whichever rings help the bridle to fit to your horse's individual anatomy. For less leverage, the reins can come up a ring.

2.15 This horse is in a *wagon wheel hackamore*, which, like the flower hackamore seen in fig. 2.14, allows for flexibility in adjustment. This model has removable shanks, to offer an option with less leverage.

2.16 Abengale is wearing a very short-shanked mechanical hackamore. The degree that the shanks are swept back, along with their shortness, means that there is almost no amplification of pressure applied to the horse's face when the reins are used.

2.17 Some hackamores feel uncomfortable to the horse, even if no one is holding the reins. We can tell by the tension seen in Colton's mouth and jaw that this rigid bar under his chin isn't a good choice for him.

2.18 This Tennessee Walking Horse works well in a long-shanked mechanical hackamore.

hands may be better off in a longer shank, because small, unintended movements won't max out the pressure of the hackamore. For the same reason, a straight shank offers more degrees of leverage than a swept-back shank. Choosing the length and shape of your hackamore shank is a balancing act, with many factors to consider.

Purchase

The *purchase* of your mechanical hackamore is the length of metal that goes from the headstall to the nose piece. A longer purchase is meant to encourage a horse to lift his head, since the longer purchase releases poll pressure. A shorter purchase-to-shank ratio is supposed to help a horse lower his head. Try different purchase-to-shank-ratio hackamores on your horse, and feel the difference in the amount of force that is felt on the poll, nose, and lower jaw with each version.

S HACKAMORE

Good For: Mild Leverage, Lightweight Stability, Mouth Clearance
Not Ideal For: Refined Cues

The S hackamore is actually a mechanical hackamore with a distinctive design. Its design allows it to be fit differently than the other mechanical hackamores I've mentioned. The metal cheeks of the *S hackamore* swoop along the sides of the horse's head and can produce a stabilizing effect. This allows the S hackamore to be effective, even if it is adjusted loosely. Note, however, that you may need shorter cheekpieces on your bridle to accomodate for the S hackamore's design. This design is a popular choice for endurance riders, because the looseness in the area of the nose and jaw allows horses to easily eat and drink and it is lightweight, yet it provides more control than a halter (fig. 2.19).

SIDEPULL

Good For: Transitioning In-Hand Cues to Ridden Cues
Not Ideal For: Situations Requiring Leverage

A *sidepull*, sometimes called a "side cue," is the mildest type of bitless bridle. There are no moving pieces in a sidepull, and the rein ring is close to the junction of the noseband and the headstall. This setup provides a 1:1 ratio between the pressure

2.19 Bella switched to an S hackamore when she had a problem with one of her premolars. The cheek of this hackamore style does not touch the skin over the first and second premolars, and has a curb strap that sits farther back on the lower jaw than hackamores with other designs.

the rider puts on the reins and the pressure that the horse feels on his nose. Severity can be increased or decreased based on the shape and the materials used in the sidepull. For example, a rounded sidepull will be more severe than a flat, wide sidepull.

Sidepull nosebands can convert bitted bridles to bitless bridles, similar to mechanical hackamores (fig. 2.20). Both mechanical hackamores and sidepull nosebands can be used in conjunction with a bit, as I did when I rode Shotgun Jack (see p. 3).

Although a sidepull is quite mild, when correctly adjusted, it may limit how much a horse can open his mouth to yawn or eat. If the sidepull is put on loose

> **Riding in a Halter Is Like...**
>
> If you are riding your horse in a halter with your reins or lead rope attached to the sides, you are essentially riding in a sidepull. If you are riding your horse in a halter with the reins or lead rope attached at the bottom ring, you are riding in a rudimentary traditional hackamore. A loping hackamore falls into the category of sidepull, since it works off direct pressure.

2.20 Risa's favorite sidepull is a lightweight, flat, and padded noseband that is attached to a standard bridle crownpiece and browband.

2.21 Rosie's favorite sidepull is integrated into a bridle with lots of padding and straps for stability.

enough for your horse's mouth to fully open, it will likely slip to the side when a single rein is engaged and pull the opposite cheekpiece into your horse's eye. Some sidepulls have added strapping to combat the slippage, like a leather brace on the top part of the noseband that extends to the cheekpiece (fig. 2.21). Jaw straps that tighten just in front of the horse's jowl also serve to minimize slippage.

CROSS-UNDER

Good For: Applies Pressure Over a Larger Surface Area
Not Ideal For: Releasing with Good Timing

Cross-under bridles have two long straps under the browband on either side of the headstall, where the throatlatch would be on a traditional bridle (figs. 2.22 and 2.23). These straps go under the horse's head, and feed through a ring on the opposite

2.22 Nico's cross-under bridle shows us several places where two pieces of leather, or leather and metal, intersect. Watch these spots for signs of skin pinching or hair pulling when the straps are in motion.

2.23 Another type of cross-under bridle, sometimes called a "double scawbrig," has two straps that cross from the noseband, go under the jaw, and then run through a ring on the noseband.

side of the noseband. The rein attaches to a ring at the end of these straps. When the rider activates a rein, the horse feels pressure on his poll, under his jaw, and the opposite side of his nose. The pressure creates a "hugging" effect for the horse.

The cross-under bridle is favored by some horses and confusing for others. The moving straps are slow to release when the rider's hand releases, which can make training more challenging. However, some horses respond well to the feeling of their head being gently squeezed.

CAVESSON

Good For: Horses That Tilt Their Heads
Not Ideal For: Horses That Prefer Lightweight Bridles or Riders Looking for a Western Aesthetic

Cavessons are most commonly used for longeing. They resemble a halter, often with a jowl strap instead of a throatlatch. A cavesson has between one and three metal

2.24 The metal rings on top of this cavesson's noseband connect to a metal plate that follows the curve of Ari's nose.

rings attached to the top of the noseband—one in the center, and often another ring attached an inch or so below and on either side of the center ring (fig. 2.24). Depending on the materials used in construction, cavessons can be lightweight or quite heavy.

Riding in a cavesson is similar to riding in a sidepull, because there are no moving pieces with a mechanical effect. However, with a cavesson, the points where you attach the reins are closer to the top of the horse's nose, which gives a different feel than a rein attached lower on the horse's jaw.

The shape, width, and weight of the metal over the noseband affects the severity of the cavesson. For example, *serretas* are a form of cavesson where the noseband has serrated metal where it touches the top of the horse's nose. The metal may or may not be covered with leather. Although *serretas* are still in use today, it is quite easy to cause pain or damage a horse's nose with this device.

Sometimes, cavessons are used in addition to a bit. In classical dressage lithographs, cavessons are often seen with a single direct rein, or a draw rein, attached, usually in conjunction with a bitted bridle.

COMBINATION

Good For: Offering a Large Range of Cues
Not Ideal For: Simplicity

Combination bitless bridles offer the horse and rider more options for cues than other styles, because they have a sidepull element that works without moving parts or leverage, and a leverage element that amplifies the pressure the horse feels. The rider uses two sets of reins, similar to riding with two bits in a double bridle, with each rein carrying responsibility for different cues. There are two ways to think of the roles for each set of reins. The first is the mindset that one rein is for gentle pressure, and the other is for amplifying that pressure in the case of an emergency. Alternatively, the rider might think that one set of reins is for moving the horse's head and neck in one way, and the other set of reins is for moving the horse's head and neck in another (lateral and longitudinal flexion of the poll).

MODIFICATIONS

When it comes to bitless bridle choice and fit, if you notice issues or places where a bitless bridle falls short, you may be able to modify it yourself to make it more comfortable for your equine partner. For example, perhaps you are on the last hole of your cheekpieces when you attach your mechanical hackamore—in this case, you can get some smaller or larger cheekpieces for your bridle, or make more holes. Or maybe there is a redundant strap that irritates your horse. If it doesn't serve a purpose, cut it off! Consider the example illustrated in fig. 2.24 and all the changes I made to keep my horse comfortable and capable of performing her best—our goal for going bitless.

2.25 Rosie has a high peaked poll that means modification is necessary for traditional hackamore hangers to be comfortable for her. When I padded and wrapped parts of her hackamore hanger with a few wedge sponges (for applying cosmetics) and vet tape on either side of the apex of her poll, she was far more happy and willing in her bosal. This fix cost about five dollars and vastly improved Rosie's comfort in her traditional hackamore. I also put leather loops under the vet tape, which stabilized my fiador in a way that avoided sensitive spots under her ears and around her temporal mandibular joint. It may not be the prettiest looking solution, but it helps my horse feel light in my hands and happy.

PART 3

CONNECTING BITLESS GROUNDWORK TO BITLESS RIDDEN WORK

BRINGING IT ALL TOGETHER

The groundwork exercises discussed in Part I (beginning on p. 13) are the keys to unlocking your horse's softness and understanding of what you are communicating when being ridden. The bitless bridle will have a very similar feeling to the horse as what you may have practiced in a halter. Now, we are going to connect your groundwork from Part 1 to ridden training.

TRANSITIONING TO THE SADDLE

As a rider, you are responsible for your own body. This is as important without a bit as it is with one. You need to be able to follow the horse's motion with flexible hips, while at the same time engaging the strength of your core to stabilize your body. When you can do these two things consistently, it will be possible to have an independent seat and hands. Developing independence is critical; while she is riding her horse in motion, a rider with an independent seat and hands will be able to deliver clear messages to her bridle, without added "static" coming from attempts to stabilize her seat.

RIDING POSITION REMINDERS

A rider should strive to do the least amount of work possible with the reins and rely more on the seat and legs for steering, stopping, and starting the horse. Be mindful that you never lean to the side or collapse at the waist when riding. To aid with steering, you may turn your chest, like you are sitting on a bar stool and showing your necklace to the person sitting beside you. Adding some pressure with your inside leg can improve the horse's bend, and adding pressure with your outside leg can aid in making a turn sharper.

Your shoulders, hips, and heels should be aligned to have ideal balance while riding. Be careful not to grip with your legs to hold on; instead, trust gravity to hold you on your horse. Work on your core strength and hip flexibility to move with your horse. Use your energy (p. 26) to prepare and cue your horse for transitions between gaits *before* using your leg or reins. Stay tall and still on top of your horse so he can best feel your seat, especially during transitions.

When you are less reliant on your reins for steering and stopping, they can be used to perform other tasks, like influencing the flexion of the horse's poll, doing some lateral work, and helping him with his lateral and longitudinal balance.

MOUNTING BLOCK ETIQUETTE

It's important to me that any horse I'm going to ride consents to being mounted. This is part of how I stay safe in the saddle. A horse consenting to being mounted stands still at the mounting block without being held and will even lean toward me as I begin to get on. He doesn't move his haunches away from me or stand awkwardly (fig. 3.1).

Rider mindfulness at the mounting block is an opportunity to suss out how your horse is feeling. Horses that consent to be mounted are less likely to be unhappy or unwilling while being ridden. Groundwork at the mounting block is also crucial. It is the best way to take the language and relationship you have developed with your horse on the ground and transition it to ridden work. If you have a mecate on your

3.1 I could get on Rosie from this position, but the way she's keeping her haunches away from the mounting block makes me think that she doesn't actually want to be mounted. She is likely to walk off right away when I swing on or walk away just as I'm lifting my foot to put in the stirrup.

horse, you have a built-in lead rope that will help you with this. If you don't have a mecate, you might want to put your rope halter on under your bitless bridle, or attach a lead rope to it.

Practicing the following routine solves almost every common mounting difficulty, including swinging haunches away, walking past the block, not standing still, sidling away, and not coming up to the block at all. Stay on top of your mounting block, and move the horse to you, rather than getting up and down the mounting block to reposition your horse. As soon as the horse is not in the correct position to be mounted, keep his feet moving until he is in the correct position (see Part 1, p. 13, to review the exercises that teach these skills).

1 Start by sending him past the mounting block a couple of steps (fig. 3.2 A).

2 Yield his haunches away from you.

3 You may need to do a Shoulder Yield to have your horse step around the mounting block as you draw him past you in the opposite direction via Following a Feel (fig. 3.2 B).

4 Yield his haunches until he is lined up for mounting (fig. 3.2 C).

5 Have him Follow a Feel until his saddle is in the right spot for you to mount, then ask him to stop (fig. 3.2 D).

6 If he stops, lower your energy, and give him some praise and wither scratches (fig. 3.2 E). If he doesn't stop, return to Step 1.

3.2 A–E Rosie Follows a Feel to move past me (A). I am using the end of my rope to create drive so that she continues to move her feet until she has gotten into the correct position. Next I yield Rosie's haunches away from me. At the same time, I'm changing my leading hand and driving hand as I have Rosie do a Shoulder Yield and Follow a Feel to go back to the other side of my mounting block (B).

Once Rosie is on the other side of the mounting block, I ask her to yield her haunches to help her line up again (C). I switch my leading hand and driving hand again so that I can have Rosie Follow a Feel to line up to the block again (D). If needed, I could use my driving hand to help her shoulders move around the mounting block or encourage her to move forward.

This time, Rosie is ready to be mounted, so I pet her shoulders and give her happy and peaceful energy (E). She is showing relaxation with her neck down and ears out to the sides. She has lined the stirrup up exactly with my leg, without crookedness, and is leaning slightly in toward me. Mounting a horse that is in this position and frame of mind will give you a much better starting point for your ride than mounting a horse who is only half-willing to have a rider get on.

7 Take a few moments to breathe with him before mounting. If at any point during mounting he moves off again, return to Step 1.

8 Mount slowly. Abort mounting if your horse withdraws consent by moving away—and return to Step 1.

With consistency, your horse will start to understand where the release is during the mounting process, and where it feels good for him to stand.

GROUNDWORK EXERCISES BECOME RIDDEN EXERCISES

■ Poll Flexions to Ridden Flexions

The first thing I do when I mount a horse in a bitless bridle is to check out his Poll Flexions. I try to mimic the same feel to the horse as when I did this exercise on the ground; therefore, the direction I use my rein while in the saddle is very important.

1 While halted, slowly pick up on the rein and draw it in the direction of your waist. (Note: Your horse should remain halted during this exercise. If he starts to move his feet, calmly stop him, "ground" his front feet (see sidebar, p. 108), and reorganize yourself.)

> **Why Doesn't He Want Me to Mount?**
>
> If you have a horse that is difficult to mount, be sure he is not experiencing pain. Double-check that your saddle fits, the girth is adjusted to the proper tightness, and all his other equipment is comfortable for him. A general checkup with a veterinarian or bodyworker to ensure physical well-being is also recommended.

2 Hold firmly and unwaveringly until the horse turns his nose in that direction (figs. 3.3 A & B). Start with a soft amount of pressure; your horse should respond if you set up that response well in your groundwork. But if he does not answer, gradually escalate the pressure—just as you did with your groundwork.

3 As soon as he turns his nose toward the pressure, give the rein and praise. If you had to apply lots of pressure to get the horse to turn his head, repeat the process until he responds to a lighter amount of pressure.

4 Pressure and release is how you will build *softness* in your horse. Be careful not to drill your horse for too long,

3.3 A & B To check Rosie's Poll Flexion, I pick up my right rein, close my fingers, and add a little pressure (A). Rosie responds by turning her head toward the pressure. I keep my hand in the same place in space, so it does not move as Rosie starts to turn her head (B). Because my hand doesn't move, Rosie feels a release when she turns her head. This takes practice!

PART 3: CONNECTING BITLESS GROUNDWORK TO BITLESS RIDDEN WORK | 107

Grounding

There will be times when you want your horse's feet to stay still while you are doing something else. Instead of using your hands to stop him, you can use your energy to help his feet stay put. Start by trying to keep the front feet immobile:

1 Take a deep breath, and think of exhaling down through your legs. Feel the energy of your exhale travel down and out through the soles of your boots.

2 Breathe in again and continue to visualize your exhale moving down your horse's front legs. Allow it to flow out through the soles of your horse's front hooves into the earth.

This should serve to ground both you and your horse. Now your horse is prepared to keep his front feet still.

or he will start to think he's doing the wrong thing and brace against the pressure. Do several flexions on one side before switching to the other.

5 After you've mastered Poll Flexions at the halt, go ahead and try them in motion. You will not want to turn your horse's head very much while he is moving forward. Instead, make sure he is able to softly Follow the Feel of the rein as you pick it up to ask for a flexion, without allowing him to turn the rest of his body.

■ Backing Up from the Ground to Rein-Back in the Saddle

On the ground, you taught your horse to back up when he feels pressure on his nose (see p. 36). This is a great starting point for backing up under saddle (rein-back), but the cue for backing up should not end here. I've asked riders all over the world to describe their cues for backing up their horses, and I've gotten at least a dozen different answers. I'm not going to say any of them are *not* right, but some certainly seem to be more right than others.

The answer that seems most incorrect is to just pull back on the reins harder and harder, especially if the horse is braced with his head up and his back down. When you ask your horse to back up solely by using pressure on your reins, you limit yourself in what you can do in your rein back, as well as what your reins mean to your horse. Instead, you can pair your rein cue with a specific cue from your seat and legs that will indicate the direction the horse should move.

1 Start this exercise from a halt. Pick up your reins so that your horse will feel the same pressure on his nose as he did when you were backing him from the ground.

2 Keep your upper body still and in contact with your saddle, open your hip angle (sit up tall), and draw both of your legs back from your hips, keeping them slightly away from your horse's sides. Avoid the temptation to lean forward or backward.

3 As soon as your horse steps back, quickly release by giving the reins and bringing your legs back to their normal position. Once your horse understands the cue to back up, you can extend the cue over more backward steps.

4 If your horse doesn't move immediately, just wait longer. If he still doesn't move, cluck to him until he does. If your horse either pushes into the bridle and steps forward or braces his neck up and steps back, don't worry—he just guessed the wrong answer to the question you asked (fig. 3.4). You can help him find the right answer. Return to halt and if your horse starts to walk forward, add pressure on his nose to simulate the boundary your halter created during your groundwork. If your horse brings his head up, raise and widen your hands to keep the same pressure on his nose as when his head was in a more relaxed position. Chances are, your horse is raising his head to escape the feel of the bridle. If he finds the same feel on his head when it is up, it will discourage this bracing response.

5 If you continue to have trouble with the Rein-Back in the saddle, return to the ground and do the Backing Up from the Ground exercise again (p. 109). Once your horse is backing up softly on the ground and feeling sufficiently praised for it, get back on him right away. Now that he's already thinking of backing up, it is more likely he will get the right answer when he feels the ridden cue. You can also try the Rein-Back exercise while facing a fence, so that backing up seems easier and walking straight forward is difficult. As always, the immediate timing of your release, and the pause after your release, will both be key to your horse understanding the cue, versus just being pushed and pulled around.

Six Ways to Cue for Rein-Back

When combined with rein pressure, the following physical cues can signal to the horse to back up under saddle:

1 Open your hips and bring both legs back *without* adding pressure on the sides of the horse.

2 Use your legs in a different way than you do when you want the horse to go forward. For example, try "fluttering" your ankles like you would if you were trying to get your spur rowels to jingle.

3 Use your leg to pet your horse backward by stroking his hair in the direction it grows. Your legs should move at the speed you want your horse's backward steps to go.

4 Rock your hips side to side.

5 Bring both legs forward in front of the girth and squeeze.

6 Verbally ask your horse to back with a unique sound.

3.4 I am cueing Rosie to back up by opening my hip angle and bringing both my legs back. Rosie understands that she is supposed to back up, but she is not happy about it. Even though the reins don't show tension, Rosie is opening her mouth. Although this happens sometimes during training, if a certain movement is habitually met with resistance and doesn't improve, it is worth getting a second set of eyes to determine if there is something you are doing that is causing the horse to be uncomfortable. There might be something painful in the horse's body that is causing discomfort in the movement. I'm happy to report that following this, Rosie was able to Rein-Back softly and without resistance.

■ Arm Yield to Leg-Yield

In the groundwork section, we used the Arm Yield (p. 44) to teach the horse that when he feels pressure on one side of his barrel, he is supposed to move sideways away from it. We can set up this response to the leg while mounted, just like we set up the response to the arm while unmounted.

1 Start with a very gentle feel on the reins. You don't want to start by pulling, but you want the horse to quickly encounter pressure on his nose if he responds to your leg by going forward instead of sideways.

2 Next, add leg pressure with one leg only, seeking to make it feel as similar as possible to the pressure you created with your arm during Arm Yield (fig. 3.5).

3 If your horse responds by moving sideways, release the pressure and praise him.

4 If your horse tries to move forward, keep your leg pressure on and add pressure on the reins so your horse understands that going forward is not the answer. But rather than pulling straight back, flex your horse's poll until he is looking slightly in the direction of the leg you are using to create the yield. Creating this bend in your horse's body will make it easier for him to find the answer of going sideways.

5 While I prefer to start the Leg-Yield exercise at a halt to make it clear that a unilateral leg cue means to go sideways, not forward, some horses get worried about moving sideways from a standstill. For these horses, doing the Leg-Yield at a walk often makes more sense to them. If you choose to start the Leg-Yield at the walk, it's important to make sure that your horse is flexing in the direction of the leg you are going to apply. In other words, if I am going to use my right leg to move the horse left, he should be flexed (and even bent) to the right. For this reason, if I'm walking during a horse's first Leg-Yield, I will put the horse on a circle or other curved line. You will feel the horse's barrel sway back and forth slightly between your legs as he walks. Apply your leg as his barrel swings away, using the natural swing of his body to encourage the sideways movement you seek.

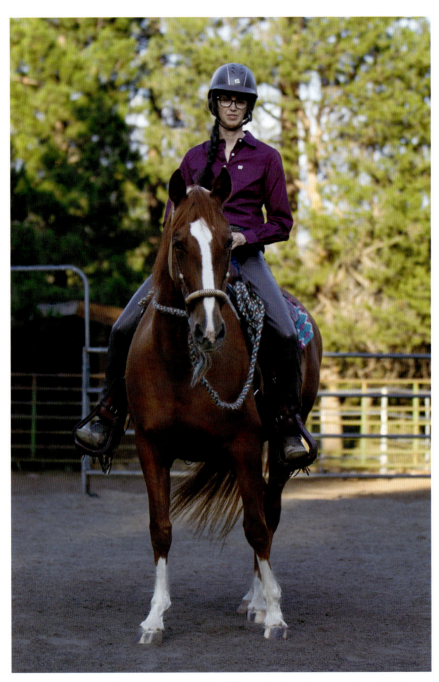

3.5 I ask Rosie to yield to my leg by making the cue feel similar to the Arm Yield she learned on the ground (p. 44).

6 When a horse can perform the Leg-Yield exercise from the halt, it is almost always easy for him to do it at the walk. If he first learns the Leg-Yield at the walk, he often will still struggle with the concept at the halt; however, he also will have a greater base of knowledge to draw on when trying to figure it out. If your horse struggles to understand the Leg-Yield at the halt for the first time, learning in the walk can help because he's already moving his legs, and the rider is changing where he puts them down. When learning at the halt, the horse needs to pick his legs up and move them sideways from the cue coming from just one leg.

■ Haunches Yield to Rein Yield

On the ground, you moved your horse's haunches solely by using the rope in your leading hand. Now, we are going to move our horse's haunches sideways from a feeling he gets from the rein. This movement will start by looking like a turn-on-the-forehand; the difference is that during the Rein Yield, you do not use your legs at all.

1 Start the Rein Yield from the halt. Make sure you and your horse are grounded as you were during the Poll Flexions (see sidebar, p. 39).

2 The direction in which you use your rein during this exercise is quite important, so your horse can distinguish between a Poll Flexion and a Rein Yield. To perform the Rein Yield, maintain a light feel on both reins, then take one hand away from your horse and up a bit, as if you were going to reach around toward the point of the horse's hip on the same side. As you move your hand far enough that the horse can see it, allow your shoulder to come back as well.

3 Your horse should immediately connect this feeling to the Haunches Yield he did in his groundwork and step his haunches away (fig. 3.6). As soon as you feel him step sideways, immediately give with your rein and praise him.

4 If your horse doesn't immediately move his hind feet, maintain pressure on the rein and wait. You may have to add more pressure, but don't vibrate, massage, or otherwise change the quality of what your horse feels. You can cluck and bring your energy up to get the horse to step sideways, but do not use your legs at all. Your goal is to teach a *rein response*, and using your leg to do the job of your rein will not serve you in the long term.

Opening Rein in a Bitless Bridle

The rein cue we are using in the Rein Yield exercise is called an *opening rein*. Some bitless bridles may swivel when an opening rein is used, digging into the horse's cheek on the side where the rein is activated. Check to see if this happens when you are testing your bridle's action and fit with your fingers (see p. 70). If your bridle digs into the horse's face when an opening rein is used, then it should only be done mildly and with mindfulness. Otherwise, it might not be the right bridle for the Rein Yield or Ridden Maestro (below) exercises.

3.6 Alex picks up her inside (left) rein, and holds her hand far enough out to the side that Quincy can see it. Quincy responds by picking up his inside (left) hind leg and crossing it over his right hind leg, resulting in a Rein Yield to the right.

5 If your horse doesn't respond softly and immediately to the Rein Yield, repeat the exercise on the same side a few times until you notice improvement. Then work on the horse's other side.

■ Maestro to Ridden Maestro

Now that your Rein Yield is functional at the halt, let's use it in motion!

1 Start on a circle at the walk. Without using your legs, take up the slack in your inside rein (inside the circle), moving your hand in the same trajectory as in your Rein Yield (see p. 113).

2 Since you've done your homework, your horse should easily step his haunches to the outside (fig. 3.7). As soon as you start to feel the haunches shift, give with your rein, continue riding forward, and praise him.

3.7 Rosie softly gives to my Ridden Maestro at the walk and abducts her right hind leg.

3 If your horse doesn't yield his haunches immediately, the trajectory of your rein cue is likely different from what he felt while standing still. Play with the trajectory and intensity of your rein cue until you get the desired response.

4 Once you and your horse are getting the feel for this cue, you can begin to minimize it. Gradually reduce how far you move your hand to the outside and the pressure you use on the rein. Try to get the desired response with as little motion in your hand as possible. Eventually, your inside shoulder coming back will be all the cue you need.

IMPROVING CONTACT AND CONNECTION

On the ground, you can develop a "diagnostic eye." You can look at your horse and decide if he needs more bend, if his neck needs to come down more, or if he needs to lift his shoulders. The exercises you've learned in this book will help adjust your horse's posture so he can travel "rounder." And as you've practiced these exercises on the ground, you've learned to take up slowly on your rope and release quickly, which builds a soft response.

But try as you might, you cannot see the whole horse while you are riding him. Therefore, you must develop a diagnostic feel to go along with your diagnostic eye. The goals stay the same—you want your horse to travel with a consistent bend and balance, and move toward a rounder frame, all with softness.

So, what does it feel like when your horse needs help with his posture?

FEELING BEND

When we talk about *flexion*, we are referring to one specific joint (the poll). When we are talking about *bend*, we are talking about the horse's whole body. When you are riding your horse, you usually want him to bend his body toward the inside of a curve, just like he does when you are longeing him. Often, people think of bend in the horse as coming from a curvature of his spine under the saddle, but this isn't biomechanically possible. Instead, to create the bend we perceive, the horse "rolls" his rib cage to the outside of the curved line. This means that when your horse lacks bend, you will feel his barrel push more firmly against your inside leg than your outside leg. Ride a figure eight and notice if your horse swings his barrel to the left and right of each circle or if he prefers to hold it consistently against one of your legs. Experiment with taking your outside leg off to see if doing so helps your horse swing his barrel over toward that leg and bend more to the inside. Use Poll Flexions and Leg-Yield (in that order) to help "roll" his rib cage away from your inside bend (fig. 3.8).

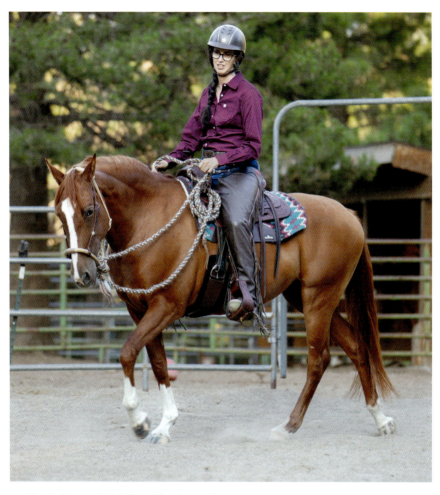

3.8 Rosie has a suitable bend for the circle we are on. Her barrel is swinging away from my left leg and toward my right leg.

Remember not to work too hard. You shouldn't keep your inside leg on constantly to create a bend. Doing so will result in a horse that pushes back against the leg. Instead, use your inside leg when his ribs are swinging slightly away from you. Once you get a response, take your inside leg slightly off the horse to see if he can hold the bend on his own. If he can't, ask him again with the same timing and release. A consistent bend is very helpful to your horse in learning to become round. But if your horse has too much bend, you will lose lateral balance.

◼ Shifting Lateral Balance

Unsure of the state of your horse's lateral balance? Try this exercise:

1 While walking on a circle, flex your horse's poll and bend his neck to the inside; his weight will go onto his inside front leg.

2 Now, counterbend him (perform a Poll Flexion and turn his neck toward the outside of the circle) and you will feel his weight move onto the other front leg.

3 Slowly reposition his neck straight, and feel his balance become equal across his front feet. Now you can feel *lateral balance*!

Use this exercise often to assess lateral balance in all gaits. Your goal is to have your horse balanced evenly over his front feet, with a slight poll flexion to the inside of the bend.

FEELING ROUNDNESS

Do you know that feeling when you are riding and your horse is about to poop, and he lifts the saddle up with his back? You might also feel his back lift right before he coughs. When your horse is correctly engaging his muscles and lifting his back, it creates a sensation for the rider similar to these two experiences all the time (fig. 3.9). But how do we encourage the horse to move this way?

Often, your horse will lower his neck to lift his back. Because lifting the back and lowering the neck go together so well, you can use Ridden Neck Lowering in order to lift the back!

◼ Ridden Neck Lowering

Use this exercise if your horse's back is down and his eyes are higher than his withers. Be sure that your horse understands Neck Lowering on the ground (p. 56) before you begin. If he can't do this with a handler on the ground, it is going to be very difficult for him to do it while balancing a rider.

1 Use the Ridden Maestro exercise (p. 114) to get your horse's inside hind foot underneath him.

3.9 Rosie is lifting her back, lowering her haunches, and arching her neck into a round frame.

3.10 I start my Ridden Maestro by bringing my inside (left) rein to the inside of our circle so that Rosie turns her neck and sees my hand. After this moment, I will maintain my upper body position and give my inside hand slightly toward her nose to encourage her to stretch her neck down and lift her back.

2 As you finish your Maestro, ride your horse on a circle, and give slightly with your inside hand (fig. 3.10).

3 Wait about eight steps for your horse to lower his neck and lift his back. If he doesn't lower his neck within that time, repeat the Ridden Maestro. It can sometimes help if you increase the horse's energy when you are coming out of the Maestro—so long as the cue to move with more impulsion doesn't cause the horse to brace his neck up even more. Altering the size of your circle (smaller, larger) can also help.

"He Never Moves Like That When I Ride Him!"

If your horse has no trouble lifting his back in his groundwork exercises but struggles to do so when ridden, you owe it to him to check out the things that are different between ridden work and groundwork. Is your saddle, pad, or girth bothering him? Find out by doing groundwork when he is wearing his saddle, and see if you have the same problem. Follow up with a visit from your veterinarian or bodyworker to look for possible physical issues, as well.

Another reason your horse may feel different between unmounted and ridden work could be that he doesn't like his bitless bridle. Ride him in the same headgear that you use for groundwork. This might mean that you attach a line to your bridle (although note that it's not appropriate to attach a line to the portion of the bridle that has leverage) or ride him in the halter that you use for groundwork, if you are comfortable doing that.

The problem could also be his rider. Be mindful that you are picking up the rein slowly and giving the release quickly, just like you've been doing in your groundwork. Check that you are balanced in the saddle, without using the reins for support. Make sure that you are riding quietly and sitting in a way that biomechanically works to everyone's advantage. Step-by-step books by professionals who focus on developing riding-specific fitness and athletic position, like *Stable Core Training* by Joyce Kramer, can help you be a more balanced partner to your horse.

FEELING LONGITUDINAL BALANCE

When your horse is round and in lateral balance, you can then improve his *longitudinal balance* by asking him to lower his haunches and elevate his withers. This is called an *uphill balance*. When you have an uphill balance, you will feel like your horse has grown taller. He should still be round, light in the bridle, and easy to turn and stop.

■ Balance Up

A horse achieves an uphill balance by lowering his haunches and raising the withers. To do this, his hind legs must take longer steps, and his front legs will take shorter steps. The Ridden Maestro (p. 114) helps develop this ability, because in this exercise, the haunches have to travel a greater distance on a circle than the front feet. This causes the horse to take big steps laterally, which can then become big steps under his body.

A

1 As you begin Ridden Maestro, be sure that you set a boundary with your outside rein. It is important now that the long step your horse takes with his inside hind leg isn't negated by an even longer step with his outside front leg. The outside front leg needs to be unwavering on its trajectory around your circle as the hind feet step out for one or two steps.

2 Decide if you would like your horse to go forward with more energy after he is Balanced Up, or if you would like for him to slow down (figs. 3.11 A & B). To come out of your Ridden Maestro with more energy, engage your core and carry your body with your energy *upward* as you ride your horse enthusiastically forward. Lighten your hands when you feel your horse carry this uphill balance so that he won't lean on you or become dull. To come out of your Ridden Maestro with a slower horse, engage your core and carry your upper body upright, while drawing your energy below your navel. Lighten your hands when you feel your horse improve his uphill

122 | SOFT, ROUND, AND BITLESS

3.11 A & B In Photo A, Risa is coming out of her Ridden Maestro with more power and uphill balance than she can carry on her own at this stage in her training. In this moment, she is leaning on my hand, but as she becomes stronger, I will be able to make frequent small releases and teach her to balance her power without so much input from me. In Photo B, Rosie is coming out of Ridden Maestro. To help slow her down and balance longitudinally, I sit tall and keep my energy low.

> **How Low Should You Go?**
>
> There is such a thing as the horse's head getting *too low*. When he is lowering his neck during stretching, try to keep his nose above his knees. When he is working in a functional frame (a posture from which he could perform a myriad of tasks without undue stress on his joints), his poll should be at least level with his withers, if not higher. Keep in mind that your horse will not be able to hold a new position for very long, just like you couldn't hold a new yoga pose for a long time on your first attempt. And always give your horse opportunities to vary his frame whenever he is being ridden.

balance so he will carry himself and not lean on the hand. An improved uphill balance will help a too-fast horse settle.

3 Remember that as you ride, rebalancing happens often. As your horse begins to understand the cues for Balancing Up, make them more subtle so that eventually your horse will rebalance in response to the position of your upper body, engagement of your core, and the location of your energy.

CARRYING ON

Whether you are training your horse on the ground or ridden, constantly check in with how you and your horse feel physically. Notice where which areas need attention, and go to your toolbox to work on those specific problems. By now, you and your horse have developed a language for communicating about bend, balance, and roundness. Strive to be a soft rider with firm boundaries, who is slow to pick up on the contact and quick to release. Keep these principles with you as you try new exercises and fun things with your horse bitless.

FREQUENTLY ASKED
QUESTIONS

MORE TO LEARN

I often hear the same types of questions from students when transitioning a horse and rider from a bitted to a bitless set up. Here are some of those questions, as well as my responses.

What's the difference for the horse (what he feels) between having a bit or going bitless?

The obvious difference for the horse between going bitted and bitless is the absence of something in his mouth. Depending on the bit, he might be interpreting signals resulting from sensations on his tongue, bars of the mouth, lips, or roof of the mouth. He might also experience pressure from the noseband as he opens his mouth. If he is wearing a leverage bit, he will also experience pressure under his jaw and over the poll.

When going bitless, the horse no longer experiences the sensations inside his mouth, but he may still feel pressure on his cheeks and teeth, depending on the adjustment of the noseband. Some bitless bridles can have leverage, causing pressure to be enacted on the lower jaw and poll. Some styles of bitless bridle offer immediate release after the rider gives a cue, and some have a delayed release effect. The elastic aspect of a horse's lips and tongue (where the effects of the bit are felt) offer different degrees of release, compared to the more rigid quality of the horse's nose (where the effects of many bitless bridles are felt).

Horses often feel more relaxed when they are bitless due to the equipment's limited effect on their expression. Many bits pull a horse's lips back, even when they are not attached to reins. How would it feel if you had someone slightly pulling your lips back all the time? Would it be distracting? Would your face get tense? Maybe try it with a friend, and see what it feels like. When helping a horse relax, we often try to put his body into a posture of relaxation. Where the body goes, the mind will often follow. When a horse pulls his lips back on his own, it is a response to stress—essentially a grimace. It seems counterintuitive to put a device on a horse that makes his face look like he is stressed, and then try to get him to relax.

What's the difference for the rider between riding with a bit and riding bitless?

Riding in a bitless bridle *properly* will make you better at riding in a bitted bridle. However, the reverse is not necessarily true—some aspects of riding well in a bitted bridle will *not* make you better at riding in a bitless bridle. I have a background in competitive dressage, and carrying a contact with the bit is mandatory. Reins are to be a straight line from the horse's mouth, all the way through the rider's forearms, to the elbow. There is never to be any prolonged drooping of the rein or void in the contact.

Usually, dressage is ridden in a snaffle bit. If we think about the surfaces that the snaffle bit works on in the horse's mouth, most are somewhat "squishy." Tongues are squishy, and lips are elastic and flexible. These squishy structures allow the horse some cushion against the rider's hand.

Horse noses are not squishy, elastic, or flexible. Therefore, carrying a constant contact on a bitless bridle does not feel the same to the horse. There is no cushion in the nasal bone or lower jaw against the rider's hand. The biggest mistake I see when riders switch to bitless bridles is they keep a steady contact like they would with a bit. Unfortunately, these riders often give up on the bitless bridle after a few rides, commenting that their horse has learned to ignore it or started to get heavy in it.

Riding bitless doesn't mean you need to ride around with your reins flapping in the breeze, but you do need to be more mindful of the contact that you carry. When you are in neutral position with your horse—not cuing him for anything in particular—you should have plus or minus .01 pounds of pressure on the reins. This means you won't have to move your hand very much to activate your reins, and your horse won't feel a steady pull on his delicate nose.

Can I go back and forth between bitted and bitless?

You bet! The exercises I've outlined in this book are the way I create a soft and round horse, regardless of headgear. The exercises work the same way as they do with a bitless bridle with most types of bits—both snaffles and curbs— so long as the bit has mobile or rotating cheeks. The light feel and contact you've developed while riding bitless will make you a better rider for riding in a bit.

When a horse goes between bitted and bitless riding, he may show a preference for one type of headgear over another, especially for a specific job. I've had horses that seemed to prefer the more granular communication of the bit over riding bitless when working on dressage. I've had horses that preferred riding in a bridleless bit over a bitless bridle. Most horses can easily go back and forth between bitted and bitless bridles.

Sometimes, riding bitless can help the horse connect better to groundwork done in the halter. Some horses like a period of bitless riding to help their mouth heal from trauma, but then accept the bit again once they have recovered. Many horses that I've started out riding bitless, stayed bitless for the rest of their riding careers.

To summarize, you might find that your horse performs certain tasks better in his bitless bridle, and certain tasks better in a bit. You can absolutely go back and forth between bitted and bitless riding. The exercises you've learned in this book to compose a common language with your horse will work the same way with a bitted bridle as they do on the ground or while riding bitless. You do not have to change the way you ride, so long as you remember to stay light in your contact.

How can I tell if my horse prefers a bitless or bitted bridle?

If you have the type of relationship with your horse where he is allowed to communicate with you just as you communicate with him, you can ask him which headgear he prefers.

Tack your horse up as usual, but when it is time to put on his bridle, bring out both his bitted and bitless bridles. Hang one bridle on each hand, take his halter off, step back, and see which bridle he brings his head to.

I often do this with my Mustang gelding, River. When I hold up both bridles, he will put his head by the one he wants to wear that day (he almost always chooses the bitless bridle). With River, I use different bridles for different tasks. If I'm on the fence about whether I should put his trail riding bridle on him or his arena work bridle, I will do the same test, put that bridle on, and then do the activity associated with it.

But if your horse isn't used to having a say in the relationship in this way, you may not get a clear answer with this method—at least, at first. Try a few days in a row, making sure you bridle him with whatever bridle he brings his head closer to. Change up which hand holds which bridle. Eventually, he should start to understand that he has a choice in which bridle he wears and show decisiveness.

If you still don't feel like you are getting a clear answer from your horse, there are other signs to look for to determine his preference. Which bridle is easier to put on? Which bridle is he more relaxed in? Which bridle is he most responsive in? All of these are ways your horse is communicating with you and are relevant pieces of information. Start to make your bridling decisions based on these factors, and your relationship with your horse will improve as he starts to feel like you are listening to him.

Should I always ride bitless? Do you?

I ride in bitless bridles, bitted bridles, bridleless bits, and sometimes, with no headgear on the horse at all. I always try to allow the horse to have a say in the type of equipment we use, but sometimes I have an occasion requiring one type of headgear over another. All horses are different, all people are different, and all relationships between the two are different. A piece of equipment that works well for me, might not be right for someone else. In my house, we have two vegetable peelers. I like the red one, and my husband likes the black one. The vegetables get peeled either way, but the experience is better for us if we each get to use the one we prefer.

I don't see bits as being inherently evil or bitless bridles as inherently good. There are plenty of bitless bridles that can cause severe damage to a horse, just as a bit can. What matters most are the hands that use the tool—and if they work with understanding, feel, and empathy for the creature on the other end of the reins.

What do I do if the horse gets heavy or hangs on my hands in a bitless bridle?

I often get asked this question by riders who carry strong contact on the reins. First, figure out if the horse is heavy on one rein or both. If he is heavy on *one* rein, review Poll Flexions (p. 106), seeking a light response both at the halt and in motion. If your horse is doing well with Poll Flexions and is heavy on the right rein, for example, use the Rein Yield (right rein) with a release at the end to get the horse to carry more weight on the right hind, and less weight in the reins. Often, a horse who is heavy on just one rein is hurting in the hind leg on the same side or he may tend to be a little lazy.

When your horse is heavy in *both* reins, first, look at your own actions—"it takes two to hang." If the rider hangs on her horse, the horse hangs on the rider. It is a cycle that only stops when someone lets go. The horse will not be the one to do this; it is always the rider who has to be the first one to release.

Next, check that you are using a hand that *holds*, not a hand that *pulls*. If you are carrying a strong contact on the rein and the horse suddenly drops the contact, does your hand stay in the same place in space, or does it move backward to maintain the contact? When the horse drops the contact and the rider's hand stays in the same place (see p. 107), she is using the desirable *holding hand*. But if the rider's hand moves backward when the horse drops the contact, she has a *pulling hand*, and the horse won't be able to find a release and develop lightness until the rider's arm control improves.

Sometimes, a horse is heavy in both reins because he needs to carry more weight on the hind legs in order to lighten the forehand. Helping this horse improve both his lateral and longitudinal balance will help him distribute his weight more evenly across his legs and improve the feel in the hand (see p. 63 for exercises to improve balance).

If you ultimately aren't successful in getting your horse to be light in a bitless bridle, you can always go back to using a bitted bridle. Riding needs to be enjoyable for the horse and the rider, so the two of you should agree on the equipment you use.

Can I compete in a bitless bridle?

It depends! I like to show in Cowboy Dressage and Working Equitation, and currently in the United States, you can compete in these disciplines using certain bitless bridles on any age of horse at any level. Show jumping, gymkhana, endurance, and certain types of trail competitions are generally also open to bitless riding. Some disciplines only allow horses of a certain age to go bitless. Other disciplines, like traditional dressage, do not currently allow bitless bridles, but there are people who are advocating for that to change. You should always read the rule book of any discipline that you compete in (this is a good idea no matter what), but particularly if you are hoping to compete bitless.

CONCLUSION

For me, bitless riding has gone from the most casual of ridden activities, to the activity that epitomizes good equitation. Bitless riding has opened my eyes to how many of the behaviors and challenges I had with riding and training were the result of a horse who was uncomfortable with his equipment. I could buy and try the gamut of bits available, but regardless of the price point, the materials, or construction, still have a horse who wasn't settled carrying a bit.

Learning to use a traditional hackamore made it easier for me to find true partnership with many clients' horses, because they weren't preoccupied with a foreign object in their mouths. I'm lucky to have a diverse enough background to be able to apply the same principles to other styles of bitless bridles and disciplines.

- I hope that more horse people will start to accept and try out bitless riding.

- I hope that more disciplines and governing bodies abandon the requirement for horses to compete with a bit.

- I hope that more horsemen will become more empathetic about what it must feel like for the horse to wear different kinds of headgear.

- I hope that this empathy leads to understanding, and that the horse will be able to have a say in what equipment he wears.

ACKNOWLEDGMENTS

It takes a village to complete a book project, and I am very grateful to everyone who helped me.

Kathy Colman Photography was responsible for most of the photos. Hollie Cower took the photos of Risa. Maria Marriott Photography shot the photo of Johnny Bug.

A number of landowners graciously allowed us to work on their property: Webb Ranch, Sage Bourassa, Carol Pauli, Kristine Hegglin.

Thanks to the women who trusted me to borrow their horses or equipment: Kate Little, Jenny Chapman, Wendy Kitchell, Jeni Rangel.

My photo models were Ruby Nuñez, Alex Rowe, and Melinda Prosser.

I'm grateful to everyone I learned from in the process of making the book. I called out Phil Monaghan and Ellen Eckstein by name, but I also was able to share things I learned from Sarah Vernlund, Sandra Beaulieu, Heather Koernemann, Bruce Sandifer, Mariko Pillitterri, Dixie Snyder, and Jody Ambrose. I'm sure there are more—please know that I'm grateful to all of you.

Gina Lohman was a stranger to me and is now the namesake of my horse skull. Bonnie McCurdy put me up. Ellie Rizol and Dr. Darren Hawks helped with beta testing. Daniel Nunez gave me physics and formatting lessons.

The sidepull in the cover image was sponsored by Anne Knightly of Royal Legacy Custom Leather. Mary Prosser filled in whenever I needed help. Martha Cook and Rebecca Didier at Trafalgar Square Books believed in this project and made it whole.

INDEX

Page numbers in *italics* indicate illustrations.

A

Abduction/adduction, 65–66

Aids. *See also* Cues
    in halts and halting, 102–3
    from legs, 44–45, 88, 102
    for rein-back, 109, *110*
    from reins, 102–3, 108, 113–14, 121, 126, 129
    from seat, 88, 102

Anxiety, in horse, 58, 66. *See also* Tension

Are-You-Happy-In-a-Bit? test, 10

Arm Yield exercise
    described, 44–45, *45*
    uses of, 111

B

Back
    hollowing of, 38
    lifting of, 118–20, *119*, 121
    relaxation of, 58–59

Back Up exercise, 36, 38–39, *38–39*

Backing up
    in-hand, 30, 36–39, 108
    while mounted, 108–10, *110*

Balance
    base of support in, 65
    downhill, 61
    exercises for, 65–66
    longitudinal vs. lateral, 63–65
    maintaining, 56, 63
    uphill, 61, *62*, 121–24, *122–23*, 129

Bars, of mouth, 9, 125

Behavior, of horse
    during bridling, 10
    consent to being mounted, 103–4

Bend and bending
    vs. flexion, 116
    rider's feel for, 116–17, *117*

Bitless bridles
    acclimating horse to, 13
    cavessons, 96–98
    combination types, 98
    cross-under, 95–96
    cueing and, 73–74
    evaluating, 70–72, *71–72*, *91*, 121
    fit considerations, 73–75, *73–74*
    hackamores, 78–92
    history of, 5–6
    materials used for, 75
    modifying, 98, *99*
    movement/mechanism of, 75–77, 88
    opening rein and, 114
    poll flexion and, 39–42, *40–42*
    sidepull, 92–95
    weight of, 76

Bitless riding
    alternating with bitted, 127, 128
    assessing horse for, 9–11, 127
    author's early history with, 1–6
    benefits, 9–11, 131
    competition rules and, 11, 130, 131
    drawbacks of, 11–12
    horse's experience of, 125–28

Bits and bitted riding
    alternating with bitless, 127, 128
    assessing horse for, 9–11, 127
    control of horse and, 11–12
    horse's experience of, 70, 125–28
    rider's experience of, 70, *71*, 126

Blackie, 3–4

Bolting, 11

Bone spurs, 3

Bosal (noseband section), 78–82, *79–80*, *82*. *See also* Traditional hackamores

Bracing, by horse, 38, *38*, 56, 106, 108–9

Brain waves, "petting" horse with, 46

Breath and breathing
    of horse, 67, 73
    of rider/handler, 25–26, 28, 46, 49, 108
Bridling, horse's behavior during, 10

C
Californio-style bridle horse, 81
Calming signals, 66, 67
Canine teeth, 9
Cartilage, on nose, 14, 73, *73*, 126
Cavessons, 96–98, *97. See also* Nosebands
Chakras, 26
Changes of direction, on longe, 52–54,
    60–61
Chewing, as calming signal, 67
Circles
    bend and, 61
    horse's frame in, 55
    pitfalls of, 61
Combination bitless bridles, 98
Competition rules, for bitless bridle use, 11,
    130, 131
Confrontational posture, 43
Connection. *See also* Language, between
    horse and rider
    emotional, between human and horse,
      49
    through reins, 116–24, 126
Contact
    in bitted vs. bitless riding, 121, 126, 129
    development of, 116–24
    lightness of, 65, 127, 129
    problems with, 1–2
    quality of, 10, 56
Control, of horse, 1, 11–12, 92
Corners, of mouth, 9
Cowboy Dressage, 5–6, *7*, 130
Cross-under bridles, 95–96, *95–96*
"Crown" evaluation technique, for nose-
    bands, 70, *71*
Crownpiece, adjustment of, 75
Cues. *See also* Aids
    conveyed through bitless bridles, 74,
      75–77
    energy as (*See* Energy control)
    in groundwork, 14, 18–21, 31

    in longeing, 22–25, *22–24*
    pointing as, 33, *33*
Curb straps
    adjustment of, 77
    on mechanical hackamores, 89, *89*
    on S hackamores, *93*

D
"Diagnostic Eye," development of, 55, 116
Direction changes, on longe, 52–54, 60–61
Disengaging the haunches, 51
Dorrance, Tom, 4
Double scawbrig bridles, *95*
Downhill balance, 61
Draaisma, Rachaël, 67
Draw to Stop exercise, 46–48, *47–48*
Drawing, of horse
    defined, 19
    hand position for, 18–19, *20*
Dressage, 4, 126, 130. *See also* Cowboy
    Dressage
Driving hand
    in leading, 18–19, *20*
    in longeing, 23

E
Ears, bridle fit and, 75
Eckstein, Ellen, 4
Emotions, of horse, 54, 59
Endurance riding, 92, 130
Energy control
    in grounding technique, 108
    for groundwork, 25–27, 30
    for longeing, 33–35, *34–35*
    in ridden work, 102–3, 122
Engagement, of haunches, 51
Equitation, 102–3, 121, 126, 130, 131
Eventing, author's background in, 1–6

F
FAQs, 125–30
Feel, of rider
    for bend, 116–17, *117*
    development of, 116
    for longitudinal balance, 121–24, *122–23*

for roundness, 118–20

Fiadors, for bosals, *79*, 86–88, *87*

Flags, for groundwork, 17

Flexibility, of horse, 65–66

Flexion, of poll, 103, 116. *See also* Poll Flexion exercises

Flower hackamore, *90*

Follow a Feel exercise
    described, 30–32, *32*
    uses of, 58, 104, *105*

Forehand
    turns on, 113
    weight on, 61

Frame, of horse. *See also* Balance
    development of, 8–9, 118–24
    in groundwork, 55

Frequently asked questions, 125–30

G

Gesture to Go exercise
    described, 33–35, *34–35*
    uses of, 58

Girth, adjustment of, 104, 121

Grazing, 11

Grounding breaths, as praise, 46

Grounding exercise, 108

Groundwork. *See also* Longeing
    as base for ridden work, 106–15
    Backing in Hand exercise, 30, 108
    benefits of, 13
    energy control in, 25–27
    equipment for, 14–17
    Follow a Feel exercise, 30–32, *32*
    as foundation for riding, 13
    handler position in, 43
    improved by bitless riding, 127
    at mounting blocks, 104
    rope handling in, 18–21
    Stopping Together exercise, 29, *29*
    testing equipment with, 13
    Walking Together exercise, 27–28, *28*

Gymkhana competitions, 130

H

Hackamores
    competition rules and, 11, 130, 131
    evaluating, *71*, *91*
    mechanical, 88–92
    nose contact and, *80*, *82*, 88
    S style, 92
    traditional, 78–88
    uses of, 5–6

"Hakma" noseband, 5

Halters
    handler's connection to, *21*
    Poll Flexions in, 39–42
    riding in, 1, 2, 93
    selection of, 14, *15–16*

Halts and halting
    aids and, 102, 108
    in groundwork, 27, 29, *29*, 33, 46–48, *48*
    rider control and, 2

Handlers
    groundwork position, 43
    patience required of, 67

Hands. *See also* Rein aids
    in groundwork, 18–21, *20–21*
    holding vs. pulling with, 38, 129
    in longeing, 22–25, *23–24*, 33
    softening of horse to, 55–63

Hanger piece, of bosal, *79*, 81, *99*

Haunches
    engagement and disengagement of, 51
    lowering of, 121
    position of, for mounting, *103*

Haunches Yield exercise
    described, 49–50, *50*
    uses of, 104, *105*, 113

Head
    anatomy of, *15*, 73–75
    dropping of, 11–12, 61–63, 123
    effects of side reins on, 56
    raising of, 38, 58
    tilting of, 40, *41*
    tossing of, 1–2, 10

Headstalls, selection and adjustment of, 70, 73, 77

Heel knots, on bosals, 78, *79*, *82*

High Caliber ("Cal"), 1

Hind legs, activity of, 11
Holding hand, 129
Horses
 checking in with, 49
 as individuals, 46
 softness in, 6
"How are you?" check-in, 49
Hyoid bone, 11

I

Individuals, horses as, 46

J

Jáquimas, 5
Jaw
 bony growths on, 3
 leverage action on, 76–77
 locking/crossing of, 10
Johnny Bug, *7*
Jumping cavessons, 2

K

Kramer, Joyce, 121

L

Language, between horse and rider
 in groundwork, 13, 14, 18, 25–27, 30
 horse's learning of, 58, 127–28
 subtlety of, 9
 universal among disciplines, 4, 67
Language Signs and Calming Signals in Horses (Draaisma), 67
Lateral balance, 63–65, *64*, 66, 129
Lead ropes. *See also* Leading
 flapping/twirling of, 19, *21*, *23–24*, 25,
  29–30, *29*
 length of, 17
 mecates as, 78, *79*, 83–84, 86, *87*
 "rolling" of, *24*
 stiffness of, 15–17, *16*
Leading
 asking for movement, 27–38
 draw and drive, 18–19
 handler position in, 19–21, *20–21*
 moving together, 27–30

Leading hand
 in groundwork, 18–19
 in longeing, 23, *23–24*
Leaning
 on circles, *64*, 65
 by horse, on reins, 56, 129
Learning, by horse, 67
Leg aids
 Arm Yield exercise for, 44–45
 in bitless riding, 88, 102
Leg-Yield, 111–13, *112*
Leverage action
 assessment for, 76–77
 of combination bitless bridles, 98
 horse's experience of, 125
 of mechanical hackamores, 4, 89
Licking, as calming signal, 67
"Life," in energy control, 25–27
Lips, of horse, 9, 125
Longe lines, 17
Longeing. *See also* Longeing exercises
 cavessons, 96–98, *97*
 direction changes in, 52–54, 60–61
 equipment for, 15–18, 96–98
 handler position in, 22–25, *22–24*, 33
Longeing exercises. *See also* Longeing
 Arm Yield, 44–45, *45*
 Back Up, 36–39, *37–39*
 Draw to Stop, 46–48, *47–48*
 Follow a Feel exercise, 30–32, *32*
 Gesture to Go, 33–35, *34–35*
 Haunches Yield, 49–50, *50*
 Maestro, 50–52, *51–52*
 Neck Lowering, 56, 58–59, *58–59*
 Poll Flexion in Motion, 55–56, *57*
 Poll Flexions, 39–42, *40–42*
 Rainbow, 60–61, *60*
 Raising the Withers, 61–63, *62*
 Range of Motion, 65–66
 Shoo! 36, *37*
 Shoulder Yield, 43, *43*
 Shoulder Yield in Motion, 52–54, *53–54*
Longitudinal balance, 63–65, *64*, 121–24,
 122–23, 129
Loping hackamores, *71*, 93

Lungeing, term origins, 22. *See also* Longeing

M

Maestro exercise
  in groundwork, 50–52, *51–52*
  ridden, 114–15, *115*
  uses of, 58
Mecates
  configuration of, *79*, 82
  as lead ropes, 78, *79*, 83–84, 86, *87*
  management/tying of, 84–86, *84–85*, *87*
  materials/thickness of, 83–84, *83*
Mechanical hackamores
  evaluating, *72*
  examples of use of, 4–5
  parts of, 88–92, *89*, *90–91*
  types/designs of, *90–91*
  using a bit with, 93
Mellor Pen Test, 70
Metal
  on halters, 14
  sensitivity/allergies to, 9
Mounting, 103–6, *103*, *105*
Mouth
  assessment of, 9
  in bitted vs. bitless riding, 125–26
  tension in, 10
Movement
  biomechanical connection to tongue, 11
  freedom of, 10

N

Nasal bone, 14, *15*
Natural horsemanship, 4
Neck
  effects of side reins on, 56
  lowering of, 58–59, 118–19
  movement of, 56
  stretching of, 123
Neck Lowering exercise
  in groundwork, 58–59, *58–59*
  ridden, 118–20, *119–20*
  uses of, 118
Neutral position, of rider, 126

Nose
  anatomy of, 14, 73, *73*, 126
  hackamore contact with, *80*, *82*, 88
Nose piece, of mechanical hackamores, 88, *89*
Nosebands
  adjustment of, 5, 73–75, *73*, 125
  evaluating, 70, *71*
  on halters, 14
  historical examples of, 5
  materials used for, *74*, 75
  sidepull, *74*

O

Off side, leading from, 19
Opening rein, 114

P

Pain
  from bits, 2–3, 9–10, 12, 70
  from hackamores, 76
  from mounting, 104
  from nosebands, 73, *73*, 98
  resistance and, 110
Palate, assessment of, 9
Partnership, control and, 11–12. *See also* Language, between horse and rider
Patience, 67
Petting/patting
  with brain waves, 46
  as praise, 46
Point of view, sharing, 46
Pointing, as cue, 33, *33*
Poll, bridle fit and, 75
Poll Flexion exercises
  basic, 39–42, *40–42*, 106
  in Motion, 55–56, *57*
  ridden, 106–8, *107*
  uses of, 58, 103, 106, 116, 129
"Poppers," on lead ropes, 17
Praise, 46, 67
Preference, horse's expression of, 127–28, 131
Premolars, 9, 93
Pressure
  from headgear, 73–75, *73–74*

horse's response to, 31
on nose, 36
on reins, 121, 126, 129
release of, 31, *38*, 106, 109
Pressure points, 75
Pulling hand, 38, 129
Purchase (length measure), of mechanical hackamores, 92
Pushing hand, 38, *39*

R

"Rabid racoon mode," 33–35, *34–35*
Rainbow exercise, 60–61, *60*
Raising the Withers exercise, 61–63, *62*
Range of Motion exercise, 65–66
Rein aids. *See also* Contact
    in balance with other aids, 102–3
    in rein-back, 108
    tactful use of, 121, 126, 129
    yielding hindquarters to, 113–14
Rein Yield exercise, 113–14, *114*
Rein-back, 108–10, *110*
Reins, riding with two sets of, 98. *See also* Rein aids
Relaxation, 67, 125–26
Release, of pressure, 31, *38*, 106, 109
Resistance, patterns of, 38, *110*
Rewards, 46
Rib cage, "rolling of," 116–17, *117*
Ridden exercises
    based on groundwork, 13, 106–15
    for bitted as well as bitless riding, 127
    Flexions, 106–8, *107*
    Leg-Yield, 111–13, *112*
    Maestro, 114–15, *115*
    Rein Yield, 113–14, *114*
    Rein-Back, 108–10, *110*
Ridden Flexions exercise, 106–8, *107*
Ridden Maestro exercise
    described, 114–15, *115*
    uses of, 118, 120–22, *120, 122–23*
Ridden Neck Lowering exercise, 118–20, *119–20*
Riders
    energy of (*See* Energy control)

experience of bitless vs. bitted riding, 70, *71*, 126
mindfulness in, 103–4
patience required of, 67
position of, 102–3, 121, 126
self-evaluation for, 121
softness in, 6, 8, *20*, 25–26
Right side, leading from, 19
"Rolling" of longe line, *24*, 25
ROM. *See* Range of Motion exercise
Rope halters, 14, *15*
Rope handling
    in groundwork, 18–21
    for mecates, 84–86, *84–85, 87*
Roundness, of horse
    circles and, 55, 61
    defined, 6–7, *7*
    development of, *59*, 116, 127
    rider's feel for, 118–20
    using devices for, 56

S

S hackamores, 92, *93*
Saddle fit considerations, 104, 121
Saddle pads, 121
Safety
    groundwork as basis for, 14
    horse's sense of, 58, 65
    during mounting, 103
    rope handling, 20, 85–86
    Shoo! exercise for, 36
Seat, effectiveness of, 88, 102
Self-carriage, 56, 61, 66
Self-regulation, by horse, 67
Semicircles, in Rainbow exercise, 60
Serettas cavessons, 97
Shanks, on mechanical hackamores, 76–77, 89–92, *90–91. See also* Leverage action
Shoo! exercise, 36, *37*
Shotgun Jack, 1–3, *3*
Shoulder Yield exercises
    basic, 43, *43*
    in Motion, 52–54, *53–54*
    uses of, 104, *105*

Shoulders
of handler, 43
of horse, 43, 52–54, 65
Show jumping, 130
Side reins, 56
Sidepull bitless bridles, 92–95, *94*
Sidepull nosebands
case histories, 2–3, *3*
design options, *74*
uses of, 93, 98
Snaffle bits, 5, 70, 126
Snaps, on lead ropes, 15, *16*, 17
Softness
of horse, 6, *7*, 106, 127
of rider, 6, 8, *20*, 25–26
Spade bits, 81
"Spirit," of rider. *See* Energy control
Stable Core Training (Kramer), 121
Standing still
grounding exercise for, 108
for mounting, 103–4, *103*
Steering, aids in, 102–3
Sticks, for groundwork, 17
Stifle joints, 11
Stillness, of rider, 67, 108. *See also* Standing
still
Stopping Together exercise, 29, *29*. *See also*
Halts and halting
Stress, signs of, 49, 58, 66, 67, *91*
Stretching, of neck, *120*, 123
Symmetry, of horse, 65–66

T
Teeth
assessing, 2, 3–4
grinding of, 1, 10
Tension
exercises for, 56, 58–59
signs of, 49, 58, 66, 67, *91*

Thoracic sling, *62*
Timing, of pressure release, 31, *38*, 106, 109
Tongue, of horse, 9–11
Traditional hackamores
benefits of, 131
bosal section, 78–82, *79–80*, *82*
competition rules and, 11, 130, 131
fiadors, *79*, 86–88, *87*
fit considerations, 78, *80*, 81, *82*
mecate, *79*, 82–85, 83–86, *87*
movement/mechanism of, 88
parts illustrated, *79*
Trail riding competitions, 130
Training
for control, 11–12
monitoring, 124
rushing of, 67
Turn-on-the-forehand, 113

U
Uphill balance, 61, *62*, 121, *122–23*, 129

V
Verbal cues, as praise, 46

W
Wagon wheel hackamore, *90*
Walking Together exercise, 27–28, *28*
Whips, for groundwork, 17
Withers, raising of, 61–63, *62*, 121
Wolf teeth, 2, 3–4
Working Equitation competitions, 130

X
Xenophon, 5